O9-ABE-405

BITTERSWEET TASTE OF SUCCESS

Number One woman tennis champ—partner in an off-beat marriage—sportscaster on national television—Billie Jean King has come a long way in her 31 years.

But it wasn't easy. And in her candid life story she tells it like it was from her first tennis game at the age of ten to her triumph on the center court at Wimbledon and her spectacular win over Bobby Riggs in 1973. Here is her girlhood in a strict but loving middle-American family, her too-early marriage to college sweetheart Larry King, the agony of enforced separations and the joy of fleeting meetings—and the abortion that shocked adoring fans.

Here, too, are the grueling hours of practice, the punishing tournaments and one-night stands, her single-minded fight to win equal footing with men for women players—the rewarding highs and the despairing lows—the bittersweet moments when even success tasted like ashes.

BILLIE JEAN
was originally published by
Harper & Row, Publishers, Inc.

Books by Billie Jean King with Kim Chapin

Billie Jean
Tennis to Win

Published by POCKET BOOKS

 Are there paperbound books you want but cannot find in your retail stores?

You can get any title in print in **POCKET BOOK** editions. Simply send retail price, local sales tax, if any, plus 25¢ (50¢ if you order two or more books) to cover mailing and handling costs to:

MAIL SERVICE DEPARTMENT
POCKET BOOKS • A Division of Simon & Schuster, Inc.
1 West 39th Street • New York, New York 10018

Please send check or money order. We cannot be responsible for cash. *Catalogue sent free on request.*

Titles in this series are also available at discounts in quantity lots for industrial or sales-promotional use. For details write our Special Projects Agency: The Benjamin Company, Inc., 485 Madison Avenue, New York, New York 10022.

BILLIE JEAN

by BILLIE JEAN KING

with Kim Chapin

PUBLISHED BY POCKET BOOKS NEW YORK

BILLIE JEAN

Harper & Row edition published 1974

POCKET BOOK edition published July, 1975

Special acknowledgment is made to Barry Lorge, who did some of the interviews from which this book was written.

L

Standard Book Number: 671-78938-4.
Library of Congress Catalog Card Number: 73-4099.
This POCKET BOOK edition is published by arrangement with Harper & Row, Publishers, Inc. Copyright, ©, 1974, by Billie Jean King. This book, or portions thereof, may not be reproduced by any means without permission of the original publisher: Harper & Row, Publishers, Inc., 10 East 53 Street, New York, N.Y. 10022.
Front cover photo by Steven Green/Armitage.

Printed in the U.S.A.

To everyone who believes in freedom, love, and equality

Author's Note

Kim Chapin, whom I've known now for six years, has worked with me closely in writing this book, our second together. Kim has been throughout both encouraging and understanding. His help has done much to make my experience as an author exciting and satisfying.

B.J.K.

Contents

*A 32-page photo insert
appears between pages 128 and 129.*

BILLIE JEAN

1

Seven Days in January:
San Francisco, 1974

MONDAY, JANUARY 14—The first day of this year's Virginia Slims–United States Lawn Tennis Association–Women's Tennis Association pro tour, a mouthful of titles that means women's tennis is in a state of relative calm for the first time in years. Simply put, Philip Morris—that's Virginia Slims—underwrites most of our tournaments; the WTA (of which I am the very reluctant president) supplies most of the players; and the USLTA agrees to go along with the whole deal. Peace is a wonderful thing. Tennis politics have been a hassle for the players and a bore to the sports public for too many years. So I hope this arrangement lasts for awhile.

I'm in pretty good shape, too. And pleased to be here. San Francisco is the perfect place for me to begin a new season. The Civic Auditorium, where we'll play our matches, is an easy commute from my apartment in Emeryville, California, just across the San Francisco–Oakland Bay Bridge, and Larry, my husband, has said he might even be in town most of the week. I'll believe it when I see him with my own eyes. Right now he's in Los Angeles, and he's supposed to be in Dallas tonight. My schedule's pretty hectic, but in a lot of ways

The house was packed, a nice, noisy crowd that seemed to be really having a good time. Let 'em scream and shout is the way I feel about it. They certainly didn't pay their money to come and whisper to each other all night.

Larry's is even worse. He's involved daily with King Enterprises, which takes care of our business stuff, and he's also the co-founder and vice president of World Team Tennis, the intercity tennis league that will begin to play in four months. Sometimes I think he spends most of his life in an airplane. God, the hours he puts in! He's not quite twenty-nine and kids around about not making it to thirty-five, but sometimes I'm not sure if he's joking.

Fact is, we're both pretty busy, and he's got his career and I've got mine. The few moments we do have together are fantastic, but, just as important, in the past few years we've been better and better able to handle the times we're apart. I wish other people could, too; the rumors about us have been wild. Just the other day another gossip columnist said we were "in splits-ville." Not only quaintly put, but not true, not true. I don't suppose there's much I can do about stuff like that, and I've about given up trying.

I guess most people might consider our lifestyle a little odd, though. Our apartment, for instance, has a bed, a small desk, a foldout couch, a stereo, and a huge

15

painting (heavy on the blacks and grays and blues), done in thirty seconds by a friend of ours with a spray gun. That's it. No furniture, no anything else. Some people say, no roots. And I guess it does sound like something out of *Future Shock*. But migosh, we've lived like that for the last half-dozen years now. I mean, that's the way we work. No big deal.

For one reason or another, a lot of players aren't here this week. Virginia Wade's probably in London, but she doesn't play too many tournaments anyway. I understand Julie Heldman's in Houston recovering from the Australian season. She did play the Bonne Bell matches down there, a team competition between the United States and Australia; Julie's very high strung, and she gives 100 percent of herself in a team situation; something like that tends to take a lot out of her. Evonne Goolagong? I don't know. I hear different stories. Some people say she'll be over here in March to play part of our circuit; others think she's waiting until WTT gets under way in May. I'm not really disappointed. She'd certainly help the circuit, and for that reason I'd like to see her here, but I also feel strongly that we all ought to have our choice about when and where we play. Besides—good news—our tour doesn't depend on any single player any more, not as it did in 1971 and 1972. Things have changed for us—fast.

Margaret Smith Court's another story. She's home in Australia pregnant with her second child, and when I first heard that, I admit I really was disappointed. I guess she and I have been the dominant players in the game for the last twelve years or so, but we've never really gone at each other for an entire season when we've both been at the top of our games. Every time I've been really up, as I am now, she's been hurt, or pregnant, and she even retired once. And every year that she's done great, I've been sick, or injured, or trying to do too many other things besides play tennis.

Recently I've been thinking a lot about how nice it would be if she and I went at it, head to head, no excuses, in a twenty-five-match series and maybe settled things once and for all.

Last year Madge beat me three times out of four and generally played terrifically. I had a lousy year, despite winning Wimbledon again and beating Bobby Riggs in the Astrodome. It wasn't just losing to her that bothered me, but I lost to a lot of other players too, and once you've been Number One, you just don't like anything less. I'm into a lot of nontennis stuff right now. My magazine, *womenSports,* is getting off the ground; I've been talking with a Los Angeles producer about doing my own television show; and there are always a bunch of business deals floating around. Still, I don't want to forget I'm a tennis player, and until I retire from competitive tennis, that's got to be my first responsibility.

I started getting ready for this season in early December. I practically moved to Los Angeles—the weather's a little bit better there than in San Francisco that time of year—and worked out daily with other circuit players like Tory Fretz, Laura DuPont, Mona Schallau, and Julie Anthony. I also hit a lot with Tony Trabert, the former Wimbledon and United States champion who coaches a lot of the women and Kathy May, one of the top junior players in the country. Nothing fancy. Just a lot of drills—forehand and backhand crosscourts, then down the line, then a lot of half-court work for volleying and up-and-back mobility. After that I'd work on my first service—it's been lousy for a couple of years—and wind up with three or four competitive sets. Finally, at night I'd sit in a chair or lie on the floor and flail my legs around with lead weights attached to my ankles. The tennis part was fine. I love hitting that little yellow ball, even if it's just in practice. But the weights, which I'm supposed to do daily because I've had two knee operations, are just agony—the ultimate in tedium. There really has to be a good TV show handy or they'll just never get done.

But it all seems to have paid off. I'm in great shape now, and I've got no excuses. I'm hoping for a good year.

Actually, '74 has already been pretty nice. Like two weeks ago I played in a special $60,000 Spalding mixed-doubles tournament in Dallas, a kind of super tournament. Mixed doubles is by far the most exciting kind of tennis, but it's always been treated as a sort of exhibition by both the players and the spectators. I think Dallas might have changed that. Chills and thrills, packed crowds at Moody Coliseum every night, and unbelievable rallies on almost every point. I couldn't sleep the whole week, especially after my partner, old reliable Owen Davidson, and I won the thing and took home ten grand each. That's more than I earned last summer at Wimbledon for winning the singles, the women's doubles, *and* the mixed.

For opening night, the San Francisco crowds were great—over 3,000 paid—and so was the show. Rosie Casals, who's always been popular here (she lives just across the Golden Gate in Sausalito) opened it with an easy win, and then I played a young Yugoslavian named Mimi Jansovec whom I'd never even seen hit before. I asked around and was told she had a weak backhand. *Fantastic* advice. Her backhand was superb. The rest of her game was promising but not quite mature enough, and our match was over in two sets. I played well enough, although I probably overhit a lot. Just trying to get used to the court and the surroundings.

In the third match, Chris Evert, the nineteen-year-old from Ft. Lauderdale with the super ground strokes, won easily too, but I didn't see any of it. There was this two-hour meeting of the WTA board of directors in the locker room. I guess maybe things weren't going as smoothly as I thought. I really did want to see Chrissie's match. God, I hope I play her in the finals. She's another player I've hardly ever been at my best against. Sure, this is only the first tournament of the year, but a win over her now might set things up for the rest of the entire season. I can't let myself think ahead, though. It's too dangerous.

TUESDAY—Couldn't sleep last night, and that's both good and bad. I need my Z's, but I also like a late-to-bed, late-to-rise schedule when I'm playing at night. So I got up late today, saw the icebox was bare (as usual), skipped around the corner to a coffee shop for breakfast, and then got into Larry's trusty Mazda for the trip to the City and *another* WTA board meeting. We've got our problems, and the main one is lack of money. We've got the membership—around eighty—but we need the dough-re-mi before we can really become a powerful force and back up our demands for minimum prize money, more carefully planned tournament scheduling, and the like. I know this is more politics and it may be boring, but what's happening is that professional tennis players, men and women (the men through their Association of Tennis Professionals), are finally getting control of their own game from the crusty and conservative amateur-run national associations like the USLTA, which have controlled tennis, almost by default, for years. Even more significantly, we're starting to provide basic services for ourselves—such things as pension plans, health benefits, and life insurance—that are pretty much taken for granted by players in other sports. Tennis is so far behind the times in these areas, though, that sometimes I feel like a 1930s labor organizer. These may be radical ideas for tennis, but they sure aren't anywhere else.

Plain old prize money is important, too, of course. Three years ago the Slims tournaments were sixteen-entry affairs and paid a heavy $10,000 per tournament. This week's San Francisco number is the first on a fourteen-event schedule that offers $750,000—thirteen tournaments at $50,000 each and one $100,000 beauty at the end of the winter-spring season. And the draws have gone from sixteen to a minimum of thirty-two—sixty-four where the facilities permit it—and there are qualifying tournaments held before each main event. It all means that more and more women will be playing tennis seriously and while they're young, because they know they can make a career of it, and that the women who are already playing top tennis are sticking around longer than they did ten, or even five, years ago. From both ends, then, the caliber of tennis is getting stronger and stronger. There's no such thing as a first-round pushover anymore. Sometimes I wish we still had a few.

Karen Hantze Susman, who was my first doubles partner back in 1961 and 1962, is here and she said this afternoon she's amazed at how many outstanding younger players there are today—quite an admission for somebody who really got her game together early. Karen was about as good as she ever got by the time she was fifteen or sixteen.

Incidentally, it's interesting that Karen's back playing again. That's a direct result of the new money and opportunity. She'd been drafted by WTT and wanted to enter a couple of tournaments to see if she could still play competitively. She's thirty-one, a year older than I am, and hasn't played much serious stuff in almost ten years, but I caught the end of her first-round match today against Lesley Hunt and she hasn't changed a bit. She's still playing tough and hitting beautiful strokes, and she beat Lesley in a third-set tie-breaker. I've often wondered what would have happened to her if she hadn't retired when she did.

I got nailed at the Civic Auditorium by Monty Stickles for a radio spot—I couldn't argue since he's an ex-pro football player—and by a television crew that wanted to do a short, on-camera bit; then I escaped for a light snack with Vicki Berner, a good friend and former circuit player who's now in charge of our qualifying tournaments. After listening to Vicki trying to talk me into building a house on some land she owns in British Columbia, I dug into my fruit salad and ice cream.

I don't eat meals anymore. Four weeks ago I doubled over during one of those Los Angeles practice sessions and was rushed to the hospital for what seemed the umpteenth time in my life. The doctor asked me if I'd been under any strain recently. I just laughed. Then he ran some barium tests and told me I had either the beginnings of an ulcer or a tumor. Great. He told me to come back in six weeks and he'd share the good news with me. In the meantime, he put me on the old ulcer diet—ice cream, spaghetti, rice, and good things like that—and said absolutely no salads, no fried foods, and no beer. It's lucky I like—am passionate about—ice cream. I ought to look like a balloon when this thing's over, but so far I haven't gained a pound. I'm right about 135 and holding.

Later in the day I found out the Associated Press had named me its 1973 Sportswoman of the Year. A nice honor, but in fact if anybody in tennis deserved it in '73, Margaret Court did. On the other hand, I thought I should have won in 1971, and that time it went to Evonne Goolagong for winning the French Open and Wimbledon.

Maybe you could say things even out. But they don't, not really. I think all performers want to get their recognition at the exact moment it's due them, not two years earlier or two years later. I'm sure Margaret will always feel a little upset she didn't win in '73, and I know that for me nothing will ever really make up for not winning in '71. It's the same thing with line calls. You get screwed on one point and you get a break on the next, but it's never an even trade.

A strange thing happened back at the Auditorium after I'd finished a light workout. A woman in her early thirties with this odd, intense look in her eyes—she was almost crying—grabbed me by the shoulders and almost before I could say a word told me how she'd been forced to give up athletics when she was a teenager because of pressure from her family. She said she felt foolish even talking to me, but that I was the only idol she'd ever had in her life and she was glad that women finally had somebody of their own sex they could look up to.

I didn't know how to answer, I really didn't. I don't even know if she expected an answer. This kind of thing has happened more and more over the last couple of years and I'm always taken aback when it does. It confuses and embarrasses me because I guess I don't really understand what kind of an impact I, or my tennis, or my success, or whatever it is, has had on other women. But it sure means something to them. Maybe because I've been successful I sometimes forget how tough it is for women to even have the opportunity to succeed. Maybe, but I don't *think* so. I really feel sorry for all the women who never had the chance to develop their careers, athletic or otherwise, because they were taught to believe it was the wrong thing to do. It's really sad, and I would like to think those days are over. But I know they're not, and we have to keep creating opportunities for ourselves.

No singles tonight, but Chris Evert and I made our debut as a doubles team and won easily over Karen Krantzcke and Wendy Overton. My partnership with Rosie Casals might be over—it's too early to tell for sure—but whatever happens it's no big deal. We're sort of like a music group that decides to break up just because they're tired of working with each other every day. I mean, I liked playing with Rosie, and we were tremendously successful, but in a way we weren't really the ideal team. Our games were too much alike. I'm aggressive and tend to play better with the more shots I get to hit, but Rosie's the same way and I'd wind up having to let her take over at net while I just concentrated on getting my returns of service in.

With Chris that isn't a problem. She's still unsure of herself at net, and while I think she'll eventually develop an adequate volley, I'm also pretty sure she'll never have a great one. With those ground strokes of hers that's the least of her worries. Tonight we only got crossed up once—on a low lob we both stumbled after and neither of us hit. Not bad for the first time out.

WEDNESDAY—A business day. Geez, this is only the first tournament of the year and already the hassles are starting. I've got an unlisted phone number at the apartment, but give it to one person and pretty soon the whole world knows. The first call, though, was legitimate. It was from Jim Jorgensen, a young CPA who joined Larry and me last summer as a partner in King Enterprises. Jim's not dumb. He took one look at Larry's schedule, and mine, and wrote into his contract that both Larry and I have to call him once a day, every day, regardless of where we are or what we're doing. Good move.

We talked for two hours and agreed to reconvene after tonight's matches. Which we did at the Jolly King, an all-night coffee shop, until 2 A.M. over my hot-fudge sundaes and dishes of ice cream.

My problem is that I've simply spread myself too thin. I turn down 99 percent of the stuff people ask me to do, but even the rest is too much. Ideally, I'd like to concentrate on just two things—WTT (I'm the player-coach of the Philadelphia Freedoms), and the new magazine, *womenSports*. All the rest I could resist more easily. I'd like to resign as president of the WTA and turn things over to some of the younger players like Rosie Casals, Mona Schallau, and others who've been involved in it almost from the beginning. And I'd like to cut down on my involvement in Tennis-America, the tennis camp setup that Dennis Van der Meer, a teaching pro, and I run. In general, I'd like to be pretty choosy about what I get involved with in the future.

Then there are the individual endorsements for companies such as Wilson (tennis rackets), Adidas (shoes), Carnation (instant breakfast), Colgate (toothpaste), and Aztec (suntan lotion). Those I can handle because they're usually one-shot deals for print ads or television spots and don't really take up a lot of time, just a day here and there. But even with arrangements like those, things are rarely as simple as they might be.

Wilson, for example. Jim Jorgensen and I spent a lot of time on that one because one of their representatives is in town and I know we're going to get into it about my contract. I've been using Wilson rackets ever since I was twelve and I've had a contract with them since 1968 when I turned pro. I love their rackets, I really do. And although Wilson has changed drastically in the past three years, I still feel they're not a progressive company, especially when it comes to women's tennis. And that I don't like at all. Basically, Wilson doesn't manufacture enough of my rackets—they always sell out before the year is over—and since I get a percentage of the wholesale price of each racket, that means not only Wilson is losing money, which is up to them, but I'm losing money too. It's quite complicated, but the only way around this that Jim and I can figure is to ask for a really large guarantee that would force them to make more rackets, just to pay off my contract. I think Wilson's going to come through, but if they don't, I'm leaving. Two or three other companies would be happy to have me, but I sure hope it doesn't come to that.

Tonight I played Betty Stove of the Netherlands in the second round and I zapped her, 6–1, 6–0. No fuss, no muss, no bother. Betty's main problem is her service, just as it is for most Europeans. A proper service swing is almost exactly like throwing a baseball, and Betty's biggest handicap is that she grew up in a place where you learn to kick things (all that soccer), not throw them. She did, in fact, boot one ball into the grandstand and got a nice round of applause.

My service, on the other hand, was super, I have to admit. I got almost 75 percent of my first serves in, a fantastic percentage, and I'm beginning to believe that for the first time in years I've got a really reliable, hard first serve. That goes along nicely with a wicked slice service I've always had—one that draws my opponent way off to the side, especially in the deuce court. Even if I don't use the slice all that much, knowing that I have it gives 'em something to think about.

THURSDAY—The morning was shot for a nice reason, for a change. Larry flew in from Dallas late last night and was waiting for me at the apartment. We disconnected the phone and, just to make sure, hid it in a closet under some pillows. We were incommunicado until noon.

Larry brought some sad news from the Big D. Rod Laver, who may be the best tennis player ever, was up a set in a tournament against Cliff Richey and then—El Foldo. He missed a couple of shots he shouldn't have tried to make, then let up on one he should have gone for, and it was all over.

When I was in Dallas earlier this month I talked to Rod and really urged him to go for just one more big year before he had to retire. For a minute I could see the old fire in his eyes—when Rod gets psyched up his eyes turn green and almost vicious—and then it was gone. Rod's problem is simple: he's got an ego and he's stubborn, he's too damned stubborn. He thinks he should split the lines on every shot he hits and win every tournament he enters. That's the right attitude to have, of course, but he's got to be somewhat realistic. He's thirty-five and he's got to realize he can't go for the lines on every shot, and even more important, that there are a lot more good players now than there were even four or five years ago when he did win everything he entered. If Rod wins seven tournaments in 1974— say ten tournaments—that would be the same as winning twenty-five or thirty in 1968 or '69. He's got to adjust because if he doesn't, he's dead. God, I hate to even hear about him losing, especially like that.

A relatively quiet afternoon for a change, and then I skipped a champagne reception for the press and players—can't stand those things—to have dinner with Larry at a Polynesian place near the Auditorium. Called Raffle's, if you can believe that. I tried to order something new with a name I didn't recognize but decided to pass after I found out it was dolphin. How can anybody eat a dolphin?

Larry and I got off on a long discussion about the lousy deal girls are still getting in interscholastic sports, something that he and I have talked a lot about lately. It's unbelievable. In 1971 there were 300,000 girls in the entire country in high school sports; in 1973 there were 800,000. Quite a jump until you remember how small the base figure is. In the same period, boys' participation went up only 100,000 but from something like 3.7 million to 3.8 million. It's the same old story. Girls already outnumber boys in some "sissy" sports like archery and badminton, but by and large the opportunities just aren't there. Won't there still be lots of frustrated women like the one who talked to me Tuesday afternoon?

Mixed participation? I don't know. Larry likes the idea of men's, women's, and open competition in all sports. I'm not sure about the open part yet. I think I'd be happy, right now at least, if there were equal athletic programs in the high schools (and colleges), even if they were totally separate.

Mixed sports, though, could be something real in the future, and if it happens I'm convinced women will hold their own. People always ask me where I'd be ranked among the best men players, not just duck-walking, fifty-five-year-olds. I always answer with a question: How much time will you give me to get ready? A week? A year? A lifetime?

In the quarters tonight I played Wendy Overton, a lanky Floridian who's starting to hit pretty good again after suffering an ankle injury last year. I was sluggish —too much ice cream and not enough dolphin, maybe —and my service blew up in my face, but I still won comfortably. Glad I did. Tomorrow's semis are a guaranteed sellout, and playing in front of a full house is the greatest psych there is.

Wendy was great during the post-match interview in the little hallway outside our dressing room. A guy asked me about the resentment the other women on the tour supposedly had for me the last two or three years because I was getting all the ink and winning all that dough.

Wendy didn't miss a beat. "Now, wait a minute," she said. "Why don't you ask *me* that question? The tour's where it is today because of Billie Jean, and without her none of us would have the opportunity we've got now. As far as I'm concerned, nobody's ever resented her."

That's not exactly true, but I really appreciated her speaking up like that.

The rest of the press conference was pretty typical. They asked about my schedule for the year, my service, what I felt my best shot is, where Larry was, my feelings on the Riggs match, my feelings on Margaret's match with Bobby, the WTA, and WTT. The usual stuff, but I can't tell you how great it is to have the press come to us instead of us having to go to them. Three years ago I and a few other players would have to make the rounds of all the newspapers and radio and television stations in every city we played, just to get a mention, to explain who we were and what we were doing. It's nice to be covered now just like any other legitimate professional sport.

FRIDAY—I couldn't get to sleep again last night until real late, so didn't get up until noon and ran behind most of the day. Another WTA board meeting took up a couple of hours, but we're finally starting to get some things done. For example, the seedings (how the players are placed, planted, "seeded" in the draw so the best ones don't meet each other until the late rounds) this week were atrocious. The top four—Evert, me, Kerry Melville, and Nancy Richey Gunter—were okay, but the bottom four were completely out of line. Turns out they were arranged by a trusty USLTA computer. So we've established a point system that'll automatically determine the seedings for future tournaments. It'll run about two weeks behind, but the system will be better than using punch cards, or whatever it is they're feeding to computers these days.

Practice. I worked with Kathy Kuykendall, one of the dozen or so junior players on the tour—she's only seventeen—on her overhead, then asked Kerry Harris to help me with my first service, which had gone off so miserably last night. Kerry said I was ducking my head, not keeping my eye on the ball until I'd hit it. An old habit. I've always done that. My game depends so much on me charging the net and hitting a sharp, clean first volley that I tend to think more about it than I do my service. I've got to remember not to rush things, to take it easy. One shot at a time.

Especially tonight. I'm playing Nancy Gunter, an old rival—we've been at it for fifteen years, since our junior days—who can hit all day from the base line. Patience is everything against her.

A packed house for the semifinals; a nice, noisy crowd that really seemed to be having a good time. None of this quiet, demure stuff you find at most tennis tournaments. Let 'em scream and shout is the way I feel about it. They didn't pay their money to come and whisper to themselves all night. A four-piece, candy-striped jazz band that played during the change of games didn't hurt either.

I'm in great shape. I must be, because I only lost four games against Nancy and didn't think I played particularly well. That's one thing I've noticed, though: when I'm in shape like I am now my scores can be really impressive even though deep down I think my game is off. It's a nice, comfortable feeling that gives me a lot of confidence. Tomorrow I'll need everything. Chris Evert won her semifinal too, impressively, over Kerry Melville. Now that we're going to play each other for sure, I can finally start thinking about the match.

But not right away. A mixed bag of us—some press people, Jim Jorgensen and his wife, some tournament people, and Larry and I—adjourned to the Hippo, a lively hamburger joint on Van Ness, and talked mainly about the fantastic crowds. Through Wednesday the tournament had already grossed as much as it did all of last year, and Thursday night we bumped heads with the Golden State Warriors of the National Basketball

Association, who played at the Oakland Coliseum Arena, and won easily, 3,600 to 3,011 (thank the Warriors for some of that, however). I don't know what it is. This is Evert's first appearance in San Francisco and I know that's helped a lot. Rosie and I are both from the Bay area and I'm sure that's helped, too.

I'd like to think our tour can be successful without the top names even showing up, but I don't know. At any rate, Jerry Diamond, the promoter, was feeling flush. He said he sold the full capacity of 6,400 tonight, including about 400 general admission tickets behind posts (they were sold with the explanation but people bought them anyway). Scalpers were getting $45 for $4 general admission tickets. I love it. I love it.

I was ready for a beer but remembered my stomach and stuck to a milkshake and a bowl of chocolate fudge ice cream. Then the waiters brought a sparkler stuffed in a cupcake and sang "Happy Birthday" to me. A nice touch even if it was two months late. My gosh, I'm thirty and I don't feel a thing.

SATURDAY—I still can't get over the crowds. Tonight's finals are sold out too, but when I arrived at the Civic Auditorium around four o'clock for practice there was already a line almost three-quarters of the way around the block trying to get the last 1,000 general admission seats that were held back from the advance sale. There must have been 2,000 people in line when the box office opened, and at four tickets per person— no way. Jerry Diamond took his life in his hands and told the people at the end of the line to go home, to forget it, but most of them stayed anyway. He says he could have sold maybe 12,000 seats, but even that's a guess because the advance sale stopped three days ago.

After a twenty-minute workout with Nancy—her game is very similar to Evert's—I had dinner at Raffle's again, this time with Kristien Kemmer, the clothes horse of the tour. She's actually done some modeling. Speaking of fashion, a few days ago I was named one of the ten worst-dressed women in the world by Mr. Blackwell, the Los Angeles fashion designer. He put me in good company, though. Princess Anne, Jacqueline Onassis, Raquel Welch, and Bette Midler were also on his list. In another poll, newscaster Douglas Kiker named me "most sexy." Can't make everyone happy.

Evert.
We spun our rackets. I won the spin and chose to serve first. As I walked to the base line to begin warming up, I took one last look at the crowds milling around, not yet settled, the band, the ball boys and ball girls, the umpire and linesmen, Larry—everything. The whole atmosphere of the place. And then I tried to shut out everything and concentrate on nothing but the court, the ball, and Chrissie.

Evert looks easy to play against. She puts very little spin on her ground strokes—just a little topspin on her backhand and a little slice on her forehand. Her service is hardly awesome; she just wants to get the ball in play. One other problem is a slight lack of mobility, which has kept her from developing a really solid net game.

It's all deceptive—her ground strokes are so stunning and her anticipation so uncanny that they make up for almost all her deficiencies.

Still, I felt I had the advantage. My game is more versatile and I was sure I could adjust to her more easily than she could adjust to me. I wanted to do three things against her: play her forehand because it's the more vulnerable of her ground strokes; give her short, angled shots to her backhand because she's bothered slightly by them; and finally, give her a lot of spins—slices and topspins—to keep her off balance.

That kind of game plan, though, means I'm taking all

the risks, and she's so steady and firm off the ground I can't afford to miss anything.

I held service in the first game, 4–0. (We played under "No-Ad" scoring, which means the game points were scored "1–2–3–4" instead of "15–30–40–game." At 3–3, the next point won the game.) On Chrissie's serve, I got to 3–3 but lost the next point, and the game.

That was the pattern the entire first set. I had bad nerves. I was tighter than a drum, just remembering some of the bad matches I'd played against her in the past. It was my fault for thinking that way and it helped to keep us even through the first twelve games. I always held my service easily, and four times on her service I got as far as 3–3, but never could get the crucial service break.

The first time it happened it didn't bother me. I knew I was pushing her on her service and that was good enough. Then it happened again, and again, and *again,* and by then I was pissed off. On one of those points I played it perfectly—got to the net and waited to hit an easy volley—but she broke off a crosscourt forehand that ticked the net, bounced over my racket and landed three inches in. All I could do was shrug my shoulders and try to forget it.

At 6–all we started the best-of-nine tie-breaker. I lost the first two points on my service, won two points on hers. And then came the point that decided the match.

I served and got to the net again after a short rally. This time Chris hit a perfect lob that landed about a foot from the base line. I honestly didn't hesitate for a second. I dug for the thing, ran it down, and with my back to the net managed a sharp crosscourt flick over my shoulder that caught her flat-footed. In all modesty, it was a great shot and it kept me alive. I took the point one exchange later, and the logjam was broken.

Two more points and I had the set; I knew if I could

keep up the pressure in the second set I could win, and that's exactly what happened. I took the first four games of the set. A few minutes later it was over, 7–6, 6–2.

That broke the tension, and I could finally enjoy things for the first time all week. There was even a touch of humor a few minutes later during the introductions for the doubles final. British Motor Cars has put up a Jensen Healey for the player who gets the most combined points here and next week in Mission Viejo, California. I don't know if they were amused or not when the umpire for the doubles, Norman Brooks, referred to it as a Ford Pinto. Whatever it is, I hope I win it.

Chris and I successfully finished our debut as teammates by defeating Frankie Durr and Betty Stove in the doubles final, and then I adjourned with a small party to the Hippo to celebrate the end of a great week.

God, Larry and I got this tournament about five different ways. I won two titles and he helped with the promotion, did the color for a delayed television broadcast of tonight's matches, and we even own the court. I wish we could play every week in San Francisco.

Maybe this will be a super year. So far I'm undefeated in everything—singles, doubles, and mixed—and I've won $21,600. I know it can't last forever, but I think I'll try to enjoy it as long as I can.

SUNDAY—No way. It's a beautiful day, the kind of day San Francisco wishes it had more of, at least in the winter. I wish I could report I have a fantastic view of the Bay, but I don't, ever since they put up another apartment house in front of mine a few months ago. With a little effort, though, like out the front door, turn left, and walk about 25 feet, the panorama takes in the City on the left, Sausalito on the right, and in the middle, of course, the Golden Gate. And I can report the sun sets beneath the Golden Gate—every night.

I'd love to have the day off to just goof around before going to Los Angeles tonight, but I'm locked in my apartment doing the final taping for this book while Larry's out showing Chris Evert and Laurie Fleming the sights. When he gets back we'll probably go to Celia's, a Mexican-American place down the peninsula in San Mateo, where he'll have the B-2 special and I'll have a double order of flour tortillas with butter and wish I could eat real food again. Then to the airport for the flight south where Marilyn Barnett, my secretary, will pick me up and drive me to Palm Springs. Tomorrow there's a 7:30 call for an Aztec suntan lotion television commercial. I think I'll tell the Aztec people I've discovered that their stuff not only gives a deep, even tan, but that it's also great for dry skin and for polishing shoes. It'll blow their minds.

Okay. What do you want to know?

2

Starting from Scratch:
A Fireman's Daughter
from Long Beach

I DON'T live in the past very much. In fact, I hardly live there at all. My memory is just awful for things that happened last week, let alone what happened fifteen, twenty, or twenty-five years ago. I've never kept a diary or journal or even a scrapbook. I don't know why exactly; there just never seemed to be time. Every now and then, though, I'll run across an old newspaper clipping my parents saved, or maybe a school yearbook, and that'll trigger the memory of some experience or feeling I had many years ago. I rarely remember details —what I was wearing or what somebody said to me or even whether the sun was shining (although since I grew up in Long Beach, it probably was)—and I'm sure that the few things I do remember vividly are colored by the way I feel about them now, today. Still, certain incidents stand out, and they're important to me, at least right at this moment. How important they were to me when they actually happened, I don't really know.

I was born on November 22, 1943 (at 11:30 A.M. for all you astrology freaks), and my mother says I was

I was wearing a blouse and a nice pair of tennis shorts mom had made for me. Neat, but Perry Jones had this rule: Little boys wore shorts and little girls wore dresses, and that was that.

----

a perfect child, just a little angel. Somehow I can't picture myself as a little angel—ever—but I'm happy to take her word for it. I always felt older than other kids my own age in grammar school, and I felt I was more serious about life. That's probably because I developed early physically and for a few years was always the biggest kid in class. I could laugh and tease around like everyone else, but deep down I felt I was going to do something with my life and really make my mark. I remember feeling that very strongly when I was in kindergarten, when I was around four or five years old. Maybe every kid has those feelings at that age—I don't know about that—but I think that a lot of what I've done comes from that early belief in myself.

I always wanted to travel, to *go* someplace. I remember distinctly in the fourth, fifth, and sixth grades that whenever we had those twenty-minute free periods I'd always go to this big map on the wall and pick out a city and say I wanted to visit there someday. I wanted to know what the people were like in those other places, to find out if they were any different from the kids I grew up with in Long Beach.

Los Cerritos Elementary School in Long Beach, California, had the wealthiest kids in the city. My family, the Moffitts, weren't exactly poor, but it always seemed as if we were struggling a little bit, while the other kids I knew had their own horses and went off on weekends to play golf or tennis at their parents' country clubs. I got along with the other kids fine; it was just that sometimes I couldn't do the things I wanted to do. I think that must have had a big influence on me. I remember feeling these other kids had a pretty soft life and that they were spoiled, not so much materially as mentally. We Moffitts were always sort of considered to be from the wrong side of the tracks. We weren't, not really, but compared to the other kids I can see how I might have felt that way. I can't honestly remember how self-conscious I was about that. Knowing me, though, probably a lot. But I came from a strong family—a very strong family—and I was always very proud of my parents. Even though our carpet sometimes had holes in it and a spring would occasionally pop up in a chair, I was never really embarrassed about things like that. But still I realized that we were different from a lot of the other families I knew.

Something happened in the fourth grade that really put me in a shell. I don't know what it was, because that entire year is pretty much a total blank—maybe the other kids started catching up to me in size—but by the fifth grade I was deathly shy. I loved to read a lot and I remember that one time I was supposed to give an oral book report on Peter Stuyvesant in front of the entire class and the whole thing was just too much. I put it off and put it off until my teacher, a Mrs. Delph, finally sent a note to my parents saying I'd get an unsatisfactory grade in reading if I didn't give that report.

My dad blew up. "No kid of mine isn't going to get through reading," he said.

"Dad, I can't do it," I said. "I get nervous and I'm scared to death."

He threatened to whomp me, but I didn't care. It was the easy way out. "You might as well kill me now," I said.

So he did spank me—good—and that was the lesson for the night: that there were certain things in life you *had* to do. Period.

The next day when Mrs. Delph called on me I thought I was gonna pass out. I stood up and croaked, "This book is about Peter Stuyvesant . . . ," and my whole body just turned to jelly. I guess I've had to learn a lot of lessons like that.

The next year I still had the same problem, but then the teacher was a Mr. Bamrick, and he understood things like that a little better. He encouraged me to talk about something I really liked, like baseball. By then I had figured it couldn't be any worse than it had been the year before, and when I spoke I found that the other kids were genuinely interested in what I was saying because I was too. I found out I was really communicating. From baseball I went on to dirigibles and everything was pretty okay after that.

That was also the year I started to play tennis and began having to deal with total strangers. Those two things—tennis and Mr. Bamrick—helped me to get out of my shell, but even today I'm still uncomfortable around people I don't know, and I don't think I'll ever get over that, not completely.

My mother, Betty, was always a creative person. She liked painting and ceramics, and made rugs for the den. My parents saved for five years so they could buy me a piano of my own, and then mom would get her old violin down from the attic so she could accompany me. It was terrible—El Squeako—but with a little work I think she could have been all right. My mom also loved to go shopping and talk about hair styles—the whole mother-daughter bit—but I always hated to do little-girl things and felt it was too bad she didn't have another girl around who might have enjoyed them more. I'd just as soon have been out in the backyard playing catch with dad.

My father, Bill, was with the Long Beach Fire Department. Being a fireman's daughter was pretty neat for a few years. I remember when I was just two or three he'd grab me by the waist and we'd slide down the pole at the firehouse together, and I remember this cat, the firehouse pet, who could slide down all by herself. Dad loved being a fireman and never even made a big effort for advancement, just so he could continue doing what he liked doing best—working as an engineer on all those trucks and pumping equipment.

Dad loved his job, but I sometimes think he really should have been a coach because he was an unbelievable stickler on fundamentals and discipline. When I was four years old I remember he'd spend hours playing catch with me. Dad said he couldn't afford a baseball bat, but he got a piece of wood and carved one for me, and I thought it was the greatest thing in the world. He'd sit down and pitch to me by the hour while I tried to connect with that homemade bat. I didn't do too badly.

My brother Randy—the only other little Moffitt—was born in 1948, when I was five, and dad started to work with him too as soon as he was old enough. When I started to play tennis, Randy was about six, and our household was a mess. Randy was practicing his pitching even then (he's now with the San Francisco Giants), and during the day I'd walk around with my tennis racket and try to practice my serve without knocking over too many lamps. Mom used to say that if people looked in the windows they'd think we were all crazy. If they'd looked in the backyard, their guess would have been confirmed. Any time of day when I wasn't in school, I was out there banging a tennis ball up against an old wooden fence. Eventually I literally demolished it, and dad had to build a new one for me out of cement blocks. He also put up a spotlight so I could hit after dark, which I did regularly. At night, mom and dad had their own thing. They'd go to the den dad had built and turn on the record player and dance to the Big Band sounds of people like Glenn Miller and Tommy Dorsey, while Randy and I sat on the floor and watched them. They were really lovey-dovey that way. And they still are.

I guess I was a tomboy in those years, although I wish there were a better word to describe little girls who happen to like sports. I loved to play football out in front of our house on West 36th Street, especially if I could carry the ball. I liked basketball, softball, and track too. Especially track. It was about sixty yards from this tree three or four houses down the block to another one right in front of our house, and every night after dinner dad timed all the neighborhood kids in that sixty-yard dash. I don't know how I did it without getting sick because I always used to eat like a hog.

When I was ten years old, in 1954, I was already playing on a softball team for girls fifteen years old and younger in Houghton Park, not too far from where I lived. I was shortstop, usually, and I remember one game against another public parks team in which I made a shoestring catch of a looping line drive, then spun and threw to third base to double off a runner and save the game for us in the last inning. I was mobbed when I came off the field, and later that year we won the all-city public parks championship. I was the youngest player on the team and I felt that was just about the best thing that could ever happen to me.

I loved all those sports, and I must have had some

idea that athletics was what I did best, even then, but my parents—especially my mother—weren't too keen on raising a halfback or a shortstop. One day mom ended my football career abruptly—she didn't think it was ladylike—and I guess I began to realize then there were certain sports I probably couldn't play forever.

One morning at breakfast I asked my dad what I could do, since football was out and it didn't look as if I'd be playing softball very much longer.

He thought for awhile, and finally suggested golf, swimming, or tennis.

So then I thought for awhile. Golf seemed too slow; I didn't swim very well, and besides I didn't like to spend a lot of time in the water anyway. And tennis—I really wasn't too sure what that was all about.

"Well, you run a lot and you hit a ball," dad said. "I think you'd like it."

I wasn't so sure, but I decided to give it a try.

The first problem was getting a racket. A baseball bat you could make, maybe, but a tennis racket was a whole different matter. And they were expensive, about $8 for the cheapest thing going.

But the neighbors all knew I was a sports freak, and suddenly I was doing odd jobs for everybody—a quarter here, 50 cents there—and I finally raised the dough. At least most of it. I couldn't stand the wait. "I've got to have that racket," I told mom. "I've just got to have it."

Finally, they gave in to my pestering, and one day we all went downtown and picked out a nice model with maroon nylon strings and a maroon handle. It was super.

Right away a girl in my class named Susan Williams who'd come out to California from New York asked me if I wanted to play. Of course I did. But I couldn't hit the ball at all, and I remember I was furious.

About the same time I remember watching on TV

the finals of the United States National Championships at Forest Hills, New York. I didn't know what was happening. I didn't know how to keep score or anything. But I do remember that Vic Seixas and Doris Hart won the two singles titles that year—1954—each for the first time, and that Doris especially had waited for years for that moment.

I was beginning to get turned on by the game, but I sure didn't know how to play it.

The second time I ever played tennis was the day I got my first lesson, at Houghton Park in Long Beach. It was a Tuesday in September and I wasn't quite eleven years old. I remember it was a Tuesday because the teacher was a man named Clyde Walker who worked for the city's Recreation Department and gave lessons at all the municipal parks on different days of the week; Tuesday was his day to be at Houghton Park. God, I remember everything about that day—how perfectly blue the sky was, the eucalyptus trees, and these two cement courts just sitting there.

I found out the first rule about tennis lessons the minute I stepped onto the court. I walked in, said, "Hi," and Mr. Walker replied, "Close the gate or you'll lose the whole basket of balls."

Clyde Walker was a great man. He was pretty old when I first met him—he was already in his sixties— and he was very dedicated. He'd taught in country clubs all his life, but he got out of that because he wanted to teach in the public parks, to find kids who really wanted to play. He felt the kids at the clubs weren't hungry enough, that they showed up for their lessons because their parents made them or because it was the thing to do, not because they wanted to really learn tennis and certainly not because they wanted to become champions. That first day there were three other kids, all girls, and all of them were about fourteen or fifteen.

I was already 5' 4" and weighed about 125 pounds—I haven't grown very much since—and I remember how happy he was when I told him I was only ten.

Mr. Walker showed me how to hold the racket—he taught the Continental grip—and how to drop the ball and swing through it. Then he said, "All right, Billie Jean, now you get to try it." And so I dropped the ball and swung and . . . hit it. I actually hit it, and it even went over the net. You can believe this or not, but that first day I really fell in love with tennis. With an $8 racket and some old practice balls on a public court I really sensed that tennis was going to be my sport. I stayed out there a couple of hours and I was completely enthralled, just gone in another world.

My mom finally picked me up in our 1947 Chevrolet convertible. I got into the car—I remember this so clearly—and mom asked, "How was it?"

"Great," I said. "Just great. I want to play tennis forever. I'm going to be the Number One tennis player in the whole world."

She said, "That's fine, dear," and drove me home.

I'm sure she thought this infatuation of mine would last about two weeks, but it didn't. It kept getting stronger and stronger, and I eventually gave up piano lessons so I'd have more time to play tennis and keep up my grades too. But not without a fight. For the first two years or so it was, "No piano, no tennis," until mom finally gave in. By then I was in junior high school and I'd talked my parents into driving me to all the places where Clyde Walker taught, not just Houghton Park. School got out at 3:10 in the afternoon, and by three o'clock I was so antsy I could hardly stand it.

Clyde was delighted when I started showing up at all his other classes. There was another player named Jerry Cromwell who started about the same time I did, and Clyde loved the idea that he'd finally found two youngsters who were so enthusiastic and dedicated, because, he said, he'd waited his whole lifetime for that. He spent a lot of extra time with us, even on the weekends. It paid off, because Jerry and I both were pretty successful almost right away, and we brought a lot of attention to Clyde's program. When I stopped taking lessons from him full time in 1959, five years later, all the courts in Long Beach were jammed with kids, and Clyde couldn't have been happier.

I was hardly an instant success, however. My first tournament was in December of that first year, just three months after I began taking lessons. Clyde put it together for his novice players so we could get some idea of what real competition was all about. It was quite a tournament. Clyde wouldn't even let me serve yet—I'd just drop the ball and hit a forehand to get the thing into play—because he didn't want me to worry about anything except hitting the ground strokes right. First things first. And I remember I didn't even know for sure whether balls that hit the line were good or not. I lost in the finals to my friend Susan Williams, 6–0, 6–0.

I don't think my mom and dad were ever big on tennis, but they were big on helping me as much as they could—and later, the same for Randy. My dad got by on only two pairs of shoes for eight years so we could have things, and mom worked as an Avon lady and later sold Tupperware door-to-door to bring in a little extra money. It's only been recently that they've been able to buy things for themselves. They saved for years to get some new wall-to-wall carpeting—I remember that clearly because it's all they talked about—and now they've gone overboard the other way. Every time I walk through the door of that little house on West 36th I find something new. I sometimes think that if they ever buy just one more thing, nobody'll be able to get through the door. That house is their castle, though, and over the years Randy and I have both developed a sentimental spot for it too. I've told my parents that if they ever sell their house, Randy and I will probably buy it.

I can't ever remember them having a new car, not until 1971. But dad sure knew how to buy used cars. He was a nut on them, so meticulous. Neatness counted everywhere, in fact. When he inspected our bedrooms he'd frown and say, "Well, in the Navy we had to be able to bounce a quarter on our beds." I'd laugh, but he was serious. I think maybe I've rebelled on that point.

Neatness—and discipline. Be home at a certain time, lights out at a certain time—that sort of thing. I didn't argue with either of them much when I was young. Oh, I sassed them up to a point, but then it was shape up or bend-over time. I had a pretty good temper and so did dad, but he was really funny about that. He played recreation basketball at night—and talk about determination! Mom and I watched from the stands and just waited for dad to get into one of those shouting matches with the referees, which he did a lot. And then it would happen. Somebody in the stands would see me and say, "Little girl, is that your father out there fighting?"

Mom would cringe with embarrassment, but I'd say, "Hee, hee, yup. That's my daddy." I loved it.

Dad would always get upset whenever I lost my temper, though. He always wanted me to be a good sport. "Concentrate on what you've got to do and don't make an ass of yourself like I do on the basketball court," he'd say. "I don't want you to be like me."

Many years later when he'd see me go completely bananas on the tennis court for some reason or another, I think he knew deep down what I was going through because he was so competitive himself. But he'd never admit that, not even then. The right and wrong of things were always very strong and very absolute in both my parents' minds.

I remember that security—money-in-the-bank kind of security—and the family were very important to them. They both grew up during the Depression and lived through World War II, and all of that must have had a tremendous effect on them. My mother said she remembered having only potatoes to eat because that's all her family could afford. Mom and dad always made sure that Randy and I appreciated what we had.

My father had one older sister, who died of cancer, and a younger brother, and a lot of the family responsibilities were already on his shoulders by the time he was a teenager. My father's mother left home when dad was just thirteen, and my mother had, I guess, about five stepfathers. I think that because they both came from broken homes they must have decided right from the beginning that *they* were going to have a good marriage and do everything they could to keep their own family together. They felt so strongly about giving time to Randy and me that I sometimes think they forgot about their own lives together.

The most important rule around the house was that we had to have dinner together, and it was never broken. We had to be home by 5:30 sharp or dad would go into a tirade. If we were already home the television got turned off and there were no distractions during the meal. That was the one time during the day when they'd find out what Randy and I were doing, what our thoughts were—everything.

They were pretty basic in most other ways too. Dad was the boss, the breadwinner, the one who made all the final decisions. Even though mom sure wasn't afraid to speak up, she wasn't nearly as opinionated as dad. She paid the bills and kept all the figures.

I guess my parents were prejudiced, not so much against individuals as against groups. I remember one discussion with my father about homosexuals when I was about ten. It wasn't much of a discussion, actually: he made it clear he had very little tolerance for them.

A few years later when I started going out, their first question after every date was always, "What religion is he?" And dad used to tell me, "If you ever marry a colored boy, that's the day I disown you. Don't ask me to the wedding." Yet one night when I was in college, Larry brought over a black friend and his son to visit, and my parents opened the doors and thought they were the greatest.

It was all a strange contradiction, because they brought Randy and me up to always treat each person as an individual, as a human being, but when it came down to the broader issues, I guess they were really pretty narrow.

Dad was unbelievably patriotic. He'd always stand at attention and get tears in his eyes when he heard "The Star-Spangled Banner." He believed in this country, and was pretty inflexible with people who didn't in exactly the way he did—including me. I'd suggest he had to understand that some people felt differently about the country than he did, but all he'd say was, "Goddamit. You kids don't know what we went through to make this country what it is." The standard speech. Boy, he'd get pretty irate.

My parents, dad especially, instilled in me a real desire to win, and to think big, right from the start. He always told me that if I wasn't serious about tennis, fine, but if I was, to just remember that on any day of the week there was always somebody better around, somewhere. I think that was a good attitude to have. I was always tough on the court because of that, mentally tough, and from my early teens I never thought of myself as a junior player. I only thought about myself as part of the bigger world of top women's tennis.

*   *   *

I must have been a quick learner because in June, 1955, just nine months after that first lesson with Clyde Walker, he told me he wanted me to enter a tournament at the Los Angeles Tennis Club called the Southern California Junior Championships. My first sanctioned tournament—and my first contact with the United States Lawn Tennis Association and the stuffy, country club atmosphere that was such a big part of tennis in those days.

The tennis part of the tournament went pretty well. I was only eleven, but in those days all junior players had official birthdates of January 1—just like thoroughbred racehorses—and I had to play in the Girls' 13-Under singles. It was a little hectic. Because of a mixup I got to the Los Angeles Tennis Club a day late and had to play two singles matches in one day to catch up with the field. My first match was against a girl named Marilyn Hester whom I remember because she'd been ranked somewhere around sixteenth in Southern California the year before. I beat her in straight sets, but that was really no big deal—even though at the time I thought it was—because at that age, rankings just don't mean a whole lot.

My next match was against a player named Ann Zavitkovsky, and that was important because the winner of our match got to play a girl from San Diego named Karen Hantze. If I was good for my age and experience, Karen was an absolute prodigy, and I really wanted a crack at her.

Ann and I split the first two sets. This presented a problem: I'd never played more than two sets in one match in my entire life. "What do we do now?" I asked. "Nobody won."

She explained the best-of-three deal and then beat me in that third set, 9–7, and I could have cried. I had blisters all over my feet, and on the way back home to Long Beach I realized maybe for the first time that tennis wasn't all glamour, that there was going to be a lot of hard work involved too.

I was kind of awed by the Los Angeles Tennis Club. It was a pretty posh place, and I was just as impressionable as any other kid my age, but I was also vaguely uneasy about the whole setup. I couldn't really put my finger on it, but it was something like what bothered me about some of my richer classmates at Los Cerritos. I sensed most of the kids at the tournament were different from me because they had money and I didn't. They could eat at the clubhouse, but I had to bring my lunch in a paper bag—$2 for a club sandwich was outrageous. My parents were a little uncomfortable too, because they couldn't afford to go up to the bar and maybe have a drink with other parents. My dad especially never did like the country club setups where I played most of my tournaments. He would rather have been at a baseball game, chomping down on a 25-cent hot dog.

I got used to all of this after awhile, and so did mom and dad, a little, but I could never adjust completely to the exclusiveness and formality of that kind of tennis club.

And then there was Perry T. Jones, the president of the Southern California Tennis Association and at the time maybe the single most powerful person in the entire USLTA. He was a big, slightly heavy man who always wore white shirts and suspenders, and he usually had on dark sunglasses and a straw hat. He ran his association like a dictator. Jones was a terror to all of us junior players because he controlled our lives totally —where we played, how much expense money we got from his association for trips outside California, or even if we got any at all. He wasn't a mean person, just very closed-minded about a lot of things. If you didn't toe the line you could forget about being a tennis player unless you moved to another part of the country.

Jones was a stickler for neatness and court etiquette —his juniors were always the best-groomed, best-mannered players on the circuit, owing to his strong influence.

Some of that was okay, but it was the pettiness that eventually got to a lot of people. It got to me that very first tournament when he refused to let me have my picture taken along with all the other kids because I wasn't wearing a tennis dress. Geez, I'm not sure I even knew what a tennis dress was then. I was wearing a blouse and a nice pair of tennis shorts that mom had made for me and which I thought were neat, but Jones had this rule: little boys wore shorts and little girls wore dresses, and that was that.

I guess I should have been stunned and embarrassed when he kept me out of that picture, and I probably was a little bit. It's the kind of thing that can really affect you when you're just eleven. But mainly I re member feeling just the opposite, that what he'd done was so petty that it wasn't even worth getting too embarrassed about. I think I sensed without ever really being able to say it that if I ever got the chance I was going to change tennis, if I could, and try to get it away from that kind of nonsense.

For the rest of that year and the following two years I couldn't get enough tennis. I ate up everything about the game. I read about Tony Trabert and Vic Seixas, and about Doris Hart, Shirley Fry, and Maureen Connolly—all those players. And I talked about tennis to everyone who'd listen, even to our minister, who was Bob Richards, the Olympic pole-vault champion. The Reverend Bob had come to our church—the First Church of the Brethren—shortly after he'd won his first Gold Medal in 1952.

I was really religious in those years—I even considered becoming a missionary for awhile—and Richards was a marvelous pastor. He was a regular, down-to-earth guy who wasn't caught up in all the trivial things that some ministers got hung up on. Dad liked him a lot too. They'd play together in church league basketball games and after a bad call Bob might say, "Nothing like getting screwed, is there, Bill?" and dad would just crack up.

Richards was a very articulate, emotional speaker. By the end of one of his sermons I always felt everything was wonderful, that the sky would always be blue, and that I could win any tennis tournament in the world.

He'd made his own pole-vault pit beside the church and I remember I was watching him practice one day when he asked me, "What are you going to do with your life? Do you have any idea?"

I said, "I know exactly what I'm going to do, Reverend. I'm going to be the best tennis player in the world."

I was standing there with my hands in my jeans looking very scruffy and determined, and my answer must have impressed him because I've heard he's related that incident in a lot of his speeches. I remember that I was very emphatic about it.

I was getting better in a hurry, no question. I took my lessons from Clyde and played in tournaments all over the Los Angeles area, and my Southern California rankings kept getting better and better. By 1958 I was the No. 2 15-Under girl in the Southern California association. The No. 1 player was a tiny girl from San Diego named Kathy Chabot. Kathy was only 5′ 1″, steady as a rock, and by the time the 1958 season started I'd still never beaten her.

Because of my ranking I knew I had a chance to make my first trip East that year, to Middletown, Ohio, to play in the National Girls' 15-Under championship, but I also knew that before I could go I had to get permission from Perry Jones.

I asked him straight out, "Can I make the trip?"

"Only if you beat Kathy in the Southern California tournament," he said.

"If Kathy loses are you gonna send her?"

"Yes, of course."

I was furious. I had to win to make the trip, but Kathy was going, regardless. That didn't sound fair to me, but there wasn't anything I could do about it.

Our little talk took place several months before the Southern California Junior Championships—the same tournament I'd first met Jones at three years before—and for the next ten weeks I got up at 5:30 every morning and did calisthenics and jumped rope in the backyard. I was determined to beat this little Chabot squirt even if it meant hitting 15 million balls back, and I knew that's exactly what I'd probably have to do.

Well, I did beat her, in a long, long match, although the scores were nice and neat: 6–3, 6–4. And then came the problem of money.

I asked Jones for some money, but he wouldn't give me anything, and the Long Beach Tennis Patrons, a group that had been formed a few years before to help promising junior players like myself, agreed to foot the whole bill. But Jones insisted that I have a chaperone along—mom—and that meant there wouldn't be enough money for us to fly East. We'd have to take the train. And because there wasn't enough money, it also meant I wouldn't be able to play any of the other tournaments on the Eastern circuit.

It took us three days to get from California to Middletown and mom was sick the whole way. I slept like a baby. I was seeded fourth, behind Carol Prosen of Florida, Vicki Palmer of Arizona, and Kathy Chabot, but the tournament was played on Tenneco and I'd never even seen composition clay courts before—I didn't have a clue how to run on it—and I lost in the quarter finals to Carol Hanks of St. Louis.

Those are the facts, which I know because I looked them up. What I really remember is what happened the last day of the tournament. This car pulled up to our hotel gate and about six girls got in to head off farther east to the Junior Girls' 18-Under championships in Philadelphia. After that, they would join the regular USLTA grass-court circuit for the rest of the summer. The big time.

I wanted to go so badly I had tears in my eyes and my insides literally ached. I remember standing there just completely frustrated and totally depressed. "I've got to go," I cried.

"I'm really sorry," mom said, "but we can't. We don't have any more money."

Then the car pulled away, and it just killed me.

"I'm going next year," I said to her, "even if I have to hitchhike." I was heartbroken.

Mom and I got back to Long Beach with $3 left between us.

I was ranked No. 5 in the country that year in the Girls' 15-Under—my first national ranking—and mom was delighted. She said that made the whole miserable trip worthwhile. I couldn't have cared less. The junior tournaments didn't mean anything to me, but I had wanted to play the women's events at places like Germantown and Merion and South Orange. That was one thing. And the other was that I knew a lot of the girls who had gone East weren't as good as I was; they just had the money. I vowed something like that was never going to happen again.

When I was a young teenager, everybody compared me to Alice Marble, even Clyde Walker. I guess there was good reason for it. She was a very aggressive player and had a super volley, and that's the direction my own game was taking even then. I was flattered by the comparison—who wouldn't be, since she had won at Wimbledon once, at Forest Hills four times in five years beginning in 1936, and was considered one of the greatest players of all time? But I'd never had heroines in tennis. I loved reading about and hearing about everybody, but I was sure I wanted to develop my own style, one that wouldn't remind people of anybody except me. Maybe that's one of the reasons why she and I eventually had a falling out.

In the fall of 1959, when I was sixteen, a Wilson Sporting Goods representative named Joe Bixler arranged for me to take lessons from her. I really didn't want to leave Clyde, but he told me, "It's a great opportunity. You need a lot more help than I can give you now, and Alice is a great coach. Take advantage of it."

Alice lived in Tarzana, California, about forty miles from Long Beach, and every Saturday morning my parents drove me up. Alice worked in a doctor's office until noon on Saturday, and then we'd play on a private court near her house the rest of that day and all day Sunday. Then my parents would show up again for the drive back to Long Beach.

She helped me a lot technically. She took up where Clyde had left off on the fundamentals and worked hard on the advanced aspects of shot-making, and she spotted a lot of the little flaws in my game.

What I got most from her, though, was the sense of what it was like to be a champion. She talked a lot about Don Budge, Bobby Riggs, Helen Hull Jacobs, Helen Wills Moody, and the other great players of her era. Just being around her and hearing her talk about what it was like to play championship tennis under pressure, and about winning Wimbledon and Forest Hills, really rubbed off and gave me a sense of what it would be like for me when the time came—as I was getting to know it would.

I only worked with her for three or four months, however. Alice was a sick woman. She had only one lung and she had to take oxygen every night. I'd stay at her house on Saturday nights, and when I heard her coughing in the next room it made me feel very strange.

One day she asked me straight out, "What is your goal in tennis?"

"I want to be the best tennis player ever," I said, and as soon as I did I knew immediately she wasn't going to be able to handle that. Because what I was really saying was that I wanted to be a better player than Alice Marble, even.

One weekend she called Long Beach and said she wasn't feeling well. I blurted out, "I guess that means I won't be coming up today," and she went into a rage about how selfish I was, how all I cared about were my lessons and nothing about her at all.

She finally hung up on me. I was really shaken up, especially when my parents also said I'd been selfish. I never took a lesson from Alice after that incident, but a number of years later, in 1966 when I won Wimbledon for the first time, I received a very nice note from her which I've always appreciated.

The previous summer a similar thing had happened with Maureen Connolly, whose record was even better than Alice's—three Wimbledon titles, three Forest Hills titles, the Grand Slam in 1953—just a super player. I don't even remember where it happened, but at dinner one night, just the two of us, she really laid into me. She said I was self-centered, egotistical, undedicated —just a terrible person—and that I'd never become a champion.

I couldn't believe what I was hearing. Later, I could have maybe explained away what Alice Marble said because she was sick and always a little edgy, but

Maureen was one of the nicest, most considerate people I'd ever met.

I didn't find out what was going on with Maureen until several years later. A mutual friend who'd been around both of us a lot said Maureen did believe in me—strongly—and that of all the junior players around then (this was 1959), I was the one who she felt would make it to the top. But she also knew I couldn't handle praise very well. Reverse psychology was something else, though, and so she goaded me, got my dander up. She was right on the mark, because the one way to get me to do something, even today, is to tell me I can't.

We got along fine after that night, and she made it a special point to talk to me at Wimbledon or at any other place she saw me play.

But I've always wondered, because to have two ex champions as great as Alice and Maureen blast you when you're still in your teens is pretty tough. Those two incidents left a mark on me, and I still remember them vividly. I don't think, though, that even for the right reasons, I could bring myself to say those kinds of things to a junior player.

In 1959 and 1960 I did make it East, the first year as a member of the Southern California Junior Wightman Cup team. (The Wightman Cup is the annual team competition between women from England and the United States; the Junior Wightman Cup is a team competition for girls generally eighteen years old and younger from various sections of the United States.)

It was a great two years, for a lot of reasons, and the tennis part of them completely overshadows anything I might have remembered about things like high school, or dating, or hot rods, or any of the other stuff teenage girls are supposed to remember. I was a member of a couple of school sororities, one social and one honorary, but I wasn't really into slumber parties or cars the way a lot of my classmates were. About the only thing I did with the other kids was to go to football games, which I loved. But on the weekends there was always a tournament somewhere in the Los Angeles area, and that's really where my friends came from. Back in Long Beach I kept pretty much to myself—except for Jerry Cromwell, who was almost like a second brother to me. I remember we'd walk to school together and talk about almost everything. Jerry wanted to be a Rhodes scholar, I think because he identified with Ham Richardson, a top player who had been one. Jerry almost made it—wound up with a Woodrow Wilson fellowship instead. I'd talk about a lot of dreams I had for myself and for tennis and I remember Jerry would always say, "Aw, Billie, you're just a dumb girl." And I'd answer right back, "I bet I'll change things more than you will. Wait and see."

Tennis really was becoming my whole life, almost to the total exclusion of everything else. That whole period, even the tennis, is now just a jumble of little details that I remember vividly but can't begin to put into any real chronological order.

Like eating all the ice cream in Philadelphia. In 1959 we played three tournaments in a row in the Philadelphia area, and I must have gained twenty-five pounds. I never was what you'd call svelte, but that first summer really did me in, probably forever.

Or like, that same year, seeing Forest Hills for the first time. Karen Hantze had been there before and had given me this tremendous buildup, but the first time I walked through the gate of the West Side Tennis Club, I couldn't believe how rinky-dink the place was. The grass courts in the Stadium were bad; the field courts were even worse. The dressing rooms were a mess. And those pompous USLTA officials were prancing around everywhere. The stands were never full, and it seemed as if the fans who were there couldn't have cared less.

There was just something missing emotionally, and I didn't like the whole setup at all. I lost the first match I ever played there after being up a match point, and I'm afraid that sort of set the tone for my whole Forest Hills experience.

Or like the way we lived. We were vagabonds, all of us. Most of us stayed in private homes to help cut down our expenses—I was getting travel money from the Long Beach Tennis Patrons again, a little bit from my parents, and even some from Perry Jones, but the living was never really high. We were just teenagers, though, and not too many of us cared.

Or like the people we met. On my first trip to South Orange, New Jersey, for the Eastern Grass Court Championships, a man named Frank Brennan introduced himself to me after one of my matches, took one look at the beat-up nylon in my rackets, and offered me some real gut so I could have them restrung. He later invited me to stay at his house, along with his wife and ten kids. The place was a madhouse. I remember the first time I ever ate there I was very polite and passed all the food around until suddenly there wasn't any.

"If you don't grab around here," said Mr. Brennan, "you don't eat." The next time I grabbed, and from then on I was just like one of the family.

It turned out that Mr. Brennan was a part-time tennis coach—he's since gone into teaching full time—and was absolutely great about match strategy, about small things like knowing when to lob down the line and when to lob cross court. Things like that, about which I didn't have a clue then. And for years after that he worked with me whenever I got anywhere close to New Jersey.

It was like that everywhere.

Or like the players we met. Tennis is unique, I think, in that the top players of today—at least those in their late twenties or early thirties—have literally been playing against each other half their lives or more. I first played against Maria Bueno in 1959, and the same year I also had my first match with a poker-faced Texan named Nancy Richey (later Nancy Richey Gunter), and she and I have been going at it ever since.

This period was also a very special time in American women's tennis. By 1959 most of the top players of the 1950s—people like Maureen Connolly, Doris Hart, Shirley Fry, and Althea Gibson—had already retired, and there was a tremendous vacuum at the top. We juniors were more than happy to fill it. It didn't hurt, either, that we girls from Southern California were overall the best juniors in the country, which also meant we were among the best women, period. In 1959, for example, Karen Hantze was ranked No. 6 among the women by the USLTA and I was No. 19. In 1960, Karen was No. 2, I was No. 4, and Kathy Chabot was No. 9. It was pretty heady stuff.

But mainly I remember the clubs. We played at boat clubs, cricket clubs, country clubs, and tennis clubs—everywhere. After the junior tournaments were over, the best ones among us went right to the National Clay Court Championships in Chicago, and then jumped on the USLTA grass-court circuit that led up to the U.S. Nationals at Forest Hills. If we worked things right we could play at Haverford and Germantown, both in Pennsylvania; at South Orange, New Jersey; Southampton, Long Island; Newport, Rhode Island; Brookline, Massachusetts—and finally, Forest Hills.

The whole atmosphere was very clubbish. Players traveled together, roomed together, partied together and even now and then—like Carol Caldwell and Clark Graebner, and Karen Hantze and Rod Susman—got married together.

Basically, I thought the life was great, but there was

always something in the back of my mind that kept telling me things weren't exactly the way they should be.

I found out Clyde Walker was sick in 1960, just about a year before he died. He hadn't been feeling well for some time and then there had been a lot of pain, and I remember him sitting in the sun, still trying to help Jerry Cromwell and me from his chair. Then finally he went to the hospital. His son Ted came over to the house and told us. I couldn't believe he was going to die.

The next spring, 1961, I was invited to play at Wimbledon, and I visited Clyde in the hospital just a couple of days before Karen Hantze and I were to leave for England. I told him I'd talk to him again when I got back and he said, "Yes, yes," and we both knew it was the last time we'd ever see each other.

I left for England two days before I was supposed to graduate from Long Beach Polytechnic High School. Perry Jones had recommended that Karen and I play doubles together that year and it was maybe the best advice he ever gave us. Karen and I were a great team from the start. To this day I've never had such an easy time playing doubles with anybody. Everything was a ball. We laughed a lot, just got tickled over nothing at all. And we played super. We reached the finals at Beckenham, and then won at Queen's Club, the tournament just before Wimbledon.

We weren't even seeded in doubles at Wimbledon, but I remember that Karen took one look at the draw and said, "I think we can win this thing. What about you?"

"Yeah, why not?"

But we really weren't all that confident. We'd win a match, find out when we played again, then call the airlines office and switch our flight back to the States to the following day. We did that several times until it was

61

finally Finals Day—and there we were up against Margaret Smith and Jan Lehane of Australia for the whole thing.

In the meantime, Karen and I were making a shambles out of the little room we'd rented in London. Neither of us had any money. We did our own wash, and at night our room looked like some kind of Chinese laundry with all our stuff scattered around to dry. We ate terribly. We got by on Wimpyburgers and Mars bars and that's about all—except for breakfast.

Our landlady was a Mrs. Gordon, who wasn't too crazy about having a couple of teenage girls around to begin with and was pretty cool when we first moved in. She was supposed to serve us breakfast, but on the first day it wasn't anything more than a roll and a glass of milk. Then we won our first match. The next day, orange juice. Then we won another match. Orange juice and a piece of bacon. By the start of the second week we were up to orange juice, bacon and eggs. By Finals Day the kitchen was ours, and Mrs. Gordon was absolutely cooing over "her girls" as we headed off to play.

By then, the combination of those huge breakfasts and about a hundred Mars bars made it almost impossible for me to button my skirt, but Karen and I were so absolutely loose and casual against Smith and Lehane that we beat them in straight sets. Just walked away with it, and I think if we'd stayed around an extra day Mrs. Gordon might have ordered up some Beef Wellington.

So, I'd won a Wimbledon championship on my first trip ever to the tournament I loved the best, but I didn't even go to the traditional Wimbledon Ball. Neither of us did. We both vowed we'd never go unless we won the singles. Instead, the night after the finals, Bud Collins of the Boston *Globe* treated us to dinner at a little trattoria in Belgravia. Then Karen and I stayed up the rest of the night, packing and giggling.

Clyde died three days later. His wife, Louise, said the only thing that kept him going that last week was reading the newspapers and finding out we were still in the doubles. She said Clyde would talk to the doctors about Jerry Cromwell and me, about how we were the first two really good players he'd ever coached, and about how one of us was now going to win at Wimbledon. And when I did, Louise said he just about busted his buttons, he was so proud.

3

Getting It Together: College, Marriage, Tennis, Tennis, Tennis

A COUPLE of weeks after the 1961 Wimbledon championships, I was named to the United States Wightman Cup team for the first time. Although the United States had won the Cup twenty-six out of thirty-two times in the past, hardly anyone felt we had a ghost of a chance that year. Playing for the English team were Angela Mortimer, the 1961 Wimbledon champion, Christine Truman, the Wimbledon runner-up, and Ann Haydon, the current French champion. All three of their top players, in fact, had won the French title at some point in their careers, an important point because the French tournament is the unofficial clay-court championship of the world, and in 1961 the matches were being held on clay—at the Saddle and Cycle Club in Chicago.

The top three players for the United States, on the other hand, were Karen Hantze at No. 1, me at No. 2, and Justina Bricka at No. 3. None of us had won much of anything, especially not on clay, and besides, we were all teenagers. Karen was eighteen, Justina and I were seventeen. The English tennis press came over en masse to watch the slaughter. Margaret Osborne du Pont, who may have been the best team captain ever,

When Larry told dad we wanted to get married, dad just jumped all over him: "How are you going to provide for her? . . . What if she gets pregnant right away? . . . You can't live on love." The whole works.

----

didn't share their view. She took us aside before play began and told us she believed in us, even if nobody else did, and that we'd just better begin believing in ourselves. So, on that note, we went to work.

What happened was unbelievable. On the first day, Karen lost the first set of her match with Christine Truman, but then zapped her, 6–1, 6–1, in the next two, and we had our first point.

Then I played Ann Haydon in absolutely terrible weather—it was cold and blustery both days even though it was mid-August—and won in straight sets.

Finally, Karen and I easily beat Truman and Deirdre Catt in doubles in the last match of the day, and we teeny-boppers were up, 3–0.

When Justina beat Angela Mortimer in three sets in the first match of the second day, we had the four points we needed (altogether there were seven matches). It was one of the greatest upsets in Wightman Cup history, and for me it was almost as much fun as winning the Wimbledon doubles. For the first time I had represented my country in international team competition, and for the first time I had actually gotten money—expense money—directly from the USLTA. We all received plane tickets to and from Chicago and $20 per diem, and I thought that was fantastic.

For the next three years I was a part-time tennis player. I had graduated from high school in June of 1961, and the obvious next step, it seemed, was to go right on to college. So that fall I began commuting to Los Angeles State College, about eighteen miles away on the east side of Los Angeles. I really didn't think too much about not going, not that first year, anyway. Everybody who had even half-decent grades in high school went to college, didn't they? And, in fact, I didn't mind the place. The courses I took were all right, I met a lot of new people, I just loved to sit around and talk, and besides, what else was there for me to do? A lot, as it turned out, but I didn't even begin to realize that for a couple of years.

Tennis I just forgot about for the next two years. Every season my routine was the same. I'd come back to California in September after Forest Hills and maybe play a couple of tournaments on the West Coast somewhere, then just put the old racket into mothballs. I'd dig it out again the following spring, play a few weeks, go to England for the pre-Wimbledon and Wimbledon season, and fly back to the States and play our grass-court circuit. Then back to California and retirement for seven more months. It was a great life, I thought, mainly because I didn't know any better.

At the start of my sophomore year, in the fall of 1962, I moved to an apartment off campus and took a couple of part-time jobs to help pay the bills. I made $90 a month as a playground director in a park near the campus, and I also worked in the cage of the athletic department, handing out towels and equipment to the women's gym classes.

I met Larry King that fall too, through a guy named

Marcos Carriedo. Marcos was a tennis-playing friend of mine who often played bridge with Larry in the school cafeteria, and it turned out later he'd been trying to get us together for weeks. I don't know why, exactly, except he knew that we were both pretty idealistic then, and that neither one of us smoked or drank—Mr. and Miss Puritan, that sort of thing—and I guess he figured we'd be a pretty good match. I'd had boyfriends before. Let's see. In the second grade I remember a boy named Jimmy Dunbar who used to chase after me and when I'd turn around he'd give me a big, slobbery kiss. And in the sixth grade a boy named Owen Crosby used to take me to the local drugstore for milkshakes. That was a real big deal. In 1962 I was even dating a student at Berkeley, a little more seriously than I had the others, but even that one was mostly by mail and it never turned into anything. I just wasn't interested in getting involved with anybody at that time.

Anyway, Marcos spotted me one day when I was coming out of the library elevator.

"Get back in," he said. "This guy Larry King's upstairs on the third floor and you've got to meet him."

"Marcos, come on. Would you get out of here?"

"I'm serious, Billie. He's a great guy. I know you'll like him."

"What's with you? I'm not interested."

"Get in."

So we went back upstairs and into the library and walked toward the table where Larry was. He had his shoes off and he was wearing these bright red socks with his feet propped up on the chair next to him—I'll never forget the red socks—and he was reading his chemistry book. I thought, "Gee, this guy's really handsome," and I also remember how young he looked, unbelievably young. He was only seventeen, a year younger than I was, but his light, blond hair made him look even younger.

Marcos did the honors and we talked for awhile—
and that was it, the whole thing, for six months. Larry
always used to show up at the library table where I was
studying—I was on probation every other semester—
but we didn't actually go out for six months. Marcos
must have been getting worried because he set that one
up too. Our first date wasn't anything special. Larry
just came over to the house for dinner, and then we
went out dancing, but I really got the vibes early, and
after a month or so we were both pretty serious. The
first time he said, "I really like you, Billie," I *knew* it
was for real, because I'd noticed even then that those
kinds of words just didn't come that easily to him.

My parents came to like Larry a lot, but the first
meeting was, well, a little awkward. Dad whipped up
some steaks on the charcoal grill, and Larry hated
charbroiled anything. Mom whipped up this big salad,
and Larry hated salads. That was for starters.

Sometime later during the evening, dad went outside
to work in his garden, and Larry, who was a biochem-
istry major, walked out and said "What's the pH of the
soil, Bill?"

That blew dad's mind. "What's a pH?" he asked de-
fensively.

"It's a measure of how acid the soil is."

"Christ, I don't know about stuff like that. I just
know things grow or they don't grow."

After Larry left, dad said, "What's with this guy and
his p's and h's? He's gotta be a real dippy-do asking a
guy a question like that in his own backyard."

From 1961 to 1964 my tennis never got any worse,
but it never got any better, either, not really. But my
rankings sure did. I was No. 2 in the United States in
both 1963 and 1964, and in at least one world ranking
list I was No. 5 in both 1963 and 1964. I was winning
my share of singles titles on the grass-court circuit and

other places, and in international team competition I usually performed very well. I was also a member of winning Wightman Cup teams again in all three years beginning in 1962.

One of my greatest moments came in a doubles match during the finals of the first Federation Cup matches in 1963. The Federation Cup is the women's equivalent of the Davis Cup, except there are only two singles and one doubles match per contest, and all the matches between the competing countries are played within a two-week period. That first year, 1963, the matches were played at Queen's Club, London, just before Wimbledon, and Australia and the United States reached the finals. In the two singles matches, Margaret Smith defeated Darlene Hard and I beat Lesley Turner, which brought the whole thing down to the doubles match—Hard and me against Smith and Turner.

Darlene and I quickly got ourselves into a hopeless situation—down a set and 5–4 with Margaret's service coming up. Margaret reached 40–15 (double match point) and got ready to serve to me. It was an impossible position for us and Margaret knew it. She bombed her service, I mean whopped it, wide to my forehand right where the two lines intersect, and to this day I don't know how I even got my racket on the ball. But I did, and lofted a perfect lob over Lesley's head that landed an inch from the base line. It was such a super shot that Margaret, who was rushing the net, of course, didn't even try to cover it.

Next point, Darlene hit a backhand return of service that ticked the net, just a tiny bit, but enough so that Margaret mis-hit the volley into the net. That brought us to deuce and we went on to win that game. Now we were even at 5–5, but that was no help. A few games later, I fell behind on my service, 0–40, triple break point. If we'd lost that game, it probably would have meant losing the Cup. Finally, we got rolling. We won five straight points to take the game and get back into the match. That was the turning point, even though we had to go to 13–11 before winning that second set. The third set was no problem. We won it easily, we won the match, and we won the first Federation Cup ever, and it was just a super day.

But days like that, and even my rankings, sure don't tell the whole story of what was going on. By the end of 1964, even though I'd been playing internationally for four years, I still hadn't won a major singles title—far from it—and there were always two or three players around who were better than I was.

In 1962, for example, I'd beaten Margaret Smith at Wimbledon in what most people considered a stunning upset. Great, but I didn't beat her again for almost four years. At Forest Hills I always played badly, and as far as Europe and Australia were concerned, I hardly played there at all.

At this point, tennis for me was still just fun. I was young enough to get a kick out of all the traveling I did and to enjoy the circuit life more or less at face value. But things were changing. After three years of doing the part-time number, I wasn't sure that I wanted to play tennis "just for fun" anymore.

In strictly tennis terms, the problem boiled down to something pretty simple: I wanted an all-court game, to be able to hit every shot in the book and not be restricted to just one style of play. I'd sort of sacrificed my junior career to that end—I somehow managed never to win a major junior title—because I forced myself to always try and hit the right shots and not stand back on the base line and poop-ball the way so many other junior players did. Which was noble enough, but now I was starting to realize that in order to really develop an all-court game, I had to play every day of the year, and all I was doing was this four- or five-month bit between classes at L.A. State.

It didn't bother me all the time that I wasn't playing in the off season. But every time I'd pick up the paper and read about the other kids who were playing, I'd get the itch again.

In the fall of 1964, things really came to a head. I was trying to juggle my relationship with Larry, what I thought was my obligation to get a college education, and my goal to become the Number One tennis player in the world. It was getting pretty obvious that something had to give.

Then, to really put the pressure on, I got a chance to go to Australia for three months, all expenses paid, to take private lessons from Mervyn Rose, the former Australian Davis Cup doubles player. Rose, since his retirement, had built a great reputation as a coach of world-class players. Well, that really put it on the line.

And school was the first to go. I was slowly beginning to realize that—at least for me, and at that particular point in my life—college was a farce anyway. For starters, I wasn't learning anything. I was a history major, but in those survey courses where they give you twenty books to read every semester, I never finished one. I messed around. I didn't go to classes and I cut exams. For three years I just messed around and talked to people, talked and listened. It was great, but as education it was a farce. I was trying to fit into a role that just wasn't right for me. There was this idea that everybody ought to be well rounded, and that the only way you got that way was by going to college. That's probably right on, but you can't go to school full time and become a champion tennis player. And that's what I wanted to be. For me at least, the two things were physically and mentally and emotionally incompatible. It would have been better if I hadn't ever gone to college, not then anyway.

Larry realized this even more than I did. All through 1963 and 1964, in fact, we talked about it constantly, and when I was playing the circuit we'd write letters to each other about the same thing. In 1963 I played exactly two tournaments before Wimbledon. I still managed to get to the finals, and that's the first time, I think, that I really said to myself, "Hey, Billie Jean, if you ever started putting some time in on this thing, you really could go to the top." But I didn't do anything, and from then on the pressure just built up. In 1964 I got to the semifinals at Wimbledon, again with very little preparation. When I got home that fall, Larry was exasperated.

He said, "Billie, look at your record, and with practically no work. You're a great athlete and I hate to tell you, but you shouldn't be in school."

"Well, I'm not crazy about school," I said. "You know that. But I miss you when I'm away, too. I don't want to leave you."

"Do you want to be the best? Do you really want to be Number One?"

"Yes."

"Then go do your thing. We'll make it. Don't mess up on that chance."

The whole thing was tearing me up inside and I agonized about it for weeks, but finally I made my decision, and on October 31, 1964, I left for Australia.

Now I really was scared, in a strictly tennis way, because taking that step meant I was publicly declaring my intentions of becoming Number One for the first time. An American girl just didn't show up in Australia to take lessons from a great coach without somebody asking questions, even if she was in the world's Top Ten, and my only truthful answer was that I was aiming for the top, period. It was scary. I could have stayed for years right at the level I was then without ever working too hard, but now I'd committed myself, and to hear myself say that out loud was like El Choke-o. I could have fallen flat on my face.

I couldn't afford to go to Australia on my own, of course. My benefactor was a man named Bob Mitchell, an Australian tennis patron who had helped a lot of the top players. Mitchell paid for my round-trip ticket from California, and for my lessons, for no other reason than he liked tennis and liked to be around tennis players. Unbelievable; it must have cost him $5,000, and he did it just because he loved the game.

Mitchell lived in the wealthy Melbourne suburb of Toorak, and he had a court in his backyard. (Rich Australians build tennis courts by their homes almost the way Californians build swimming pools by theirs.) Merv Rose came over at nine o'clock every morning for a long private session, and in the afternoon Owen Davidson or Roy Emerson or whoever else happened to be in town came by and I'd hit with them—and let me tell you, against those guys I really learned how to defend myself.

Rose worked me over—really worked me over—for three months. He made me run a lot (I was still pretty chubby), and he remade my service and forehand entirely. On my serve he shortened my backswing and made me toss the ball higher and farther in front of me than I'd been doing, so that I'd really have to reach for the ball. I'm not very tall, and this added a tremendous amount of power to my serve once I figured out what I was doing.

On my forehand, Merv told me I was hitting the ball too close to my body and that I was swinging with my wrist laid back, which is what you do when you don't have much faith in that shot. And I sure didn't. It was always the weakest part of my game. Merv taught me to keep my racket head in front of my wrist—to hit with confidence, in other words—and on the backswing he made me do this funny thing, like sort of bring the racket back as though I were pulling a sword out of a block of stone, and then swing forward right from the hip. That meant a short backswing, or better yet, no backswing at all. The no-backswing style is the sure trademark of a Merv Rose player.

It was really a weird-looking shot I came up with, and for months and months everybody just laughed when they saw it. But Merv said not to worry, and he guaranteed results if I hit my forehand that way for six months and then went back to hitting in the way I *thought* I *used* to hit it. He was right, of course, but it cost me a few tournaments until I got things squared away.

Finally, Merv taught me percentage tennis—that is, the best shot mathematically to use in any given situation. To give just one example, he taught me why nearly every approach shot ought to be hit down the line and why nearly every putaway shot ought to be hit crosscourt. To over-simplify, you hit approach shots to places where your opponent's angle of return is the least; you try to hit winners over the lowest part of the net, which is in the middle, because that's where you have the least chance of error. Merv made me get used to thinking patterns like that, completely, but at the same time he told me, "Billie, you're a natural athlete, and I don't want you to wind up being precise and mechanical, because you're not that kind of person, but I do want you to understand the basic principles of all this, and it's going to take a while getting used to."

As a bit of homework, he made me sit down and watch other people play, which I'd never done before. I mean *really* watch them. I had to be able to tell Merv on every point what the players had done, or what they should have done, and why. I mean, when I went to bed at night I was so tired and so confused by all of this, my head felt like a basketball.

The results were hardly apparent right away. I played the Australian circuit that winter (their summer) for the first time, and equipped with my brand-new forehand, a fresh new service, and a bold new strategic out-look, I was awful. The week after Merv showed me my new service I lost to this fourteen-year-old girl. I double-faulted thirty-five times, which must be some kind of record. But I stayed with it, and it eventually paid off.

The whole experience was exhausting, but it made a more mature tennis player out of me. It was also the last basic coaching I ever got. Clyde Walker had taught me the fundamentals, Alice Marble had taught me what it was like to be a champion, Frank Brennan gave—and was still giving me—insights into particular strategies, and Merv Rose taught me a new serve, a new fore-hand, and how to think. My tennis education, as it were, was complete, although I didn't fully realize it until the next U.S. Nationals at Forest Hills, in September, 1965.

I missed Larry terribly when I was in Australia. By now we were engaged—he'd given me the ring in a Long Beach coffee shop at 2 P.M. on October 8, just three weeks before I left—and I wrote to him prac-tically every day. By the time I got back home I couldn't wait for us to get married, and we set the date for late that summer. But not before dad really gave Larry the old third degree, I mean really raked him over the coals.

Larry was working in a school laboratory as a re-search assistant then, for a pittance, and when he told dad we wanted to get married, dad just jumped all over him: "How are you going to provide for her? . . . What if she gets pregnant right away? . . . You can't live on love." The whole works.

Larry was going, "Hmmm," I was saying, "Dad, we'll manage," and dad was saying, "No. That's not good enough." On and on.

Later, when it was all over, Larry said to me, "I just

can't believe your father talked to me that way. God, if there's one thing I know about, it's work. I've been working since I was twelve." Which was true.

But Larry did go out and get a job at Sealright Pacific, a company that manufactured those cylindrical ice cream cartons (my whole life seems to revolve around ice cream), for $400 a month. Then everything was okay with dad. Larry was going to be the provider.

Larry had come from a really poor family. He was born in Dayton, Ohio, but moved with his family to Eagle Rock, in northeast Los Angeles, when he was two. His mother died when he was very young, and afterward his father, a tool-and-diemaker, remarried. Larry grew up in a household with one full sister, one full brother, two stepsisters, and one half-brother. There was never much extra money around. The Kings used to have garbanzo beans for dinner a lot—just the way my mother used to have to eat potatoes—and the ultimate treat for Larry and his brothers and sisters was a night out for dinner, even if it was just to a roadside stand for hamburgers and french fries.

Although Larry never had any money, he was always terribly proud. He could never take anything, ever. If I tried to buy him something, just a small gift, or even offer him a bite from an ice cream cone, he'd really get weird and refuse it, because of his background.

Deep down, Larry was a warm person, a softie almost, and I knew that. But somewhere in his childhood something happened that made it difficult for that part of him to come out. We talked a lot about that even before we were married. I'd always say, "Let it all hang out," but for him it was really hard. He'd present this cold face to the world even though he was churned up inside something terrible.

In many ways, Larry was just the opposite of me. He could tell you in just so many words what he thought about life, boom-boom-boom-boom-boom. Ask me and

I'd go off in about six different directions at once. But he's always known exactly which way he was going. That isn't to say he was fantastically well ordered—neither of us is—but he had a sense of purpose, and once he latched on to a project, he got totally engrossed, and in that respect he hasn't changed much at all. He was in the Army a few years ago, in boot camp. Right? And who was the only guy in the whole platoon who could find happiness in that? Larry King. He could be digging in a shitpile as high as the ceiling, just shoveling it from one side of the room to the other, and he'd be happy. Just as long as he was doing something.

He was the only guy I'd ever known who liked working twenty-four hours a day, and he couldn't sit still, just couldn't. He always had to be doing something, anything. He'd think up a new idea, carry it off, and then go on to something else. And he was the same way about problems. Sometimes I think he'd make problems for himself just so he could figure a way out of them.

He was a strange, interesting jumble of contradictions and I loved him for it. And he was very supportive. He was behind me 100 percent in what I wanted, sometimes even before I knew what it was I wanted myself.

We were married in the First Church of the Brethren in Long Beach on September 17, 1965. He was twenty years old and just beginning his senior year at Los Angeles State. I was twenty-one, and in spite of how I felt about school, I'd just re-upped for another semester too. We lived together in a little apartment in Alhambra, not far from campus, and I stayed home all that fall and winter because I thought it was really important for me to be a good wife.

Larry was just dying. He was going to school full time, of course, and he was working at the factory full time too, sometimes the swing shift but usually the graveyard shift, and I'd bring him his lunch at two o'clock in the morning. Neither of us was crazy about the way we were living, but Larry was adamant about keeping that schedule, and besides, we needed the money since I was pulling in just $32 a week from a weekend tennis teaching job in Pasadena.

When he worked the swing shift, it wasn't too bad. He'd get home by midnight and at least get some sleep. But when he worked the graveyard shift he wouldn't get home until seven in the morning and then he'd want me to stay in bed with him until he had to go to class. God, I think I was sleeping about twenty hours a day then.

That year, however, instead of retiring my racket for the school year as I'd done before, I played tennis almost every day—hard, serious tennis. Because five days before our wedding, I'd found out for sure that I really could reach my life-long goal and become the best tennis player in the world. And, ironically, it was a defeat that told me I could become Number One.

One of the things that separates a champion from just another good player is the ability to win matches. This isn't as obvious as it sounds. The fact is that on match point against them—right at the moment the whole match is on the line—the absolute best players suddenly get about three times tougher. And if their opponents keep on playing at the same pace they did to build their lead in the first place, they're just dead.

What this is all about is the killer instinct. That's the ability to raise your level of play just enough to close out a match without any fiddling around. Get 'em on the ropes and then wham 'em—*pow,* and it's all over. Certain players never develop this ability in their entire careers. They play brilliantly right up until that moment before the end, but on that last point they just flat-out choke. I mean, we all choke once in a while.

All players, whether they're champions or not, have done it, but a champion does it less than anybody else.

The killer instinct also involves the ability to recognize turning points in a match—which, incidentally, usually occur before the public thinks they do—and do something about them. Some players never understand about that either. Others are aware of the moment but can't bring off the right shot to take advantage. You've got to be able to do both, and it's sort of a mysterious thing. It involves a tremendous amount of self-awareness and an understanding of what you can get away with and what you can't. I can't really describe it any better than that. I can feel it when I'm playing, but it's very difficult to put into words.

In the summer of 1965 I really began getting my act together, except for this killer instinct thing which I only had a vague notion about. By the time Forest Hills rolled around I was playing as well as I ever had, and although I was only seeded fifth I got to the finals —for the first time—without a whole lot of trouble. I beat Ann Haydon Jones in the quarters, 16–14, 6–2, and I steam-rollered Maria Bueno in the semis.

In the finals I played Margaret Smith, who had clearly established her greatness during the three previous years. We'd played a dozen times or more, and I'd never beaten her since that first meeting at Wimbledon in 1962.

In the first eight games of the first set I played fantastically and built a 5–3 lead. I'm told I didn't miss a volley. I don't know—I wasn't counting—but I do know I was playing what I considered to be really good, basic Merv Rose-type percentage tennis.

And then the set was over, 8–6 to Smith.

In the second set, the same thing happened. I built another 5–3 lead and even got to 40–15, double set point, on my service in the tenth game. And that's as far as I got. Three games later the match was over and the title was Margaret's, 8–6, 7–5.

It should have been a devastating blow. But it wasn't, because for the first time in a major championship I began to understand what it took to win one of those things. I began to sense what it meant to have that killer instinct, to be able to go for the jugular.

At 5–3 in both sets Margaret had picked herself up and I didn't. I was trying to be so sure of everything that I just didn't cut loose and go for the kill. I should have really muscled the ball at that point, just bopped a few. Even if I'd missed, it would have been all right because it would have shown her—and me—that I was loose and confident. But I was too conservative. I wasn't free to understand why in the hell I was in that position in the first place. I'd never had such a comfortable lead in an important match before and I didn't know what to do with it. Instead of bearing down, I was thinking, "What's going on out here?"

The answer was that I'd moved to within about one step from the very top, only I didn't fully realize it—until the match was over, and then a lot of things, the kind of stuff I'm talking about now, hit me right over the head. During the trophy presentations, in fact, I realized that I could beat Margaret, and anyone else in the world too. It just came to me in a rush, as clear as a bell, and suddenly the fact that I'd lost the match didn't bother me at all.

That match was on a Sunday, and the next Friday I got married. It was quite a week. In the space of five days I'd found out for sure that I really could be Number One, and I'd also become Mrs. Larry King. At the time, I didn't see any real conflict. Larry had switched from science to pre-law by then, and in fact his application was just about to be accepted to Boalt Hall, the law school of the University of California, Berkeley. Everything was working out great, just great. We were both so young and so idealistic that neither of us had any idea what strange and sometimes difficult directions our lives would take, not because of his law career or our marriage, but because of tennis. Even though the thought of Number One was nice, I really didn't feel I'd be playing too much longer. Maybe three or four more years. Then I figured I'd retire and have my kids and settle down as the wife of a successful lawyer. I didn't really know—not quite yet—that tennis was on the verge of a series of revolutions that would change the game forever, and neither one of us had any idea what impact all of that would have on our own lives.

The next time I played Margaret Smith was in the finals of the South African Nationals in April, 1966, and I beat her easily, 6–3, 6–2. She had taken fourteen straight matches from me since that first meeting almost four years earlier, but now I felt the tide had turned.

Three months later we played again, this time in the semifinals of Wimbledon. We played on Centre Court and again I won, easily. Everything was in place. I had the shots and I had the right mental attitude, and now I was just one match away from Number One.

4

Becoming Number One:
The Early Wimbledon Years

YEARS and years before I ever went there I felt Wimbledon was a very special place. I don't feel the same about it now, not quite, but it's still the one tournament where I always want to play my very best, and I think nearly every other player feels pretty much the same way. It may sound corny to say it, but every victory, even a first-rounder, is a triumph, and every defeat is almost a personal tragedy.

The main reason, I think, is that until four or five years ago at least, Wimbledon was, more than any other tournament in the world, a players' tournament. Sure, you noticed the pink and blue hydrangeas that were fairly recent show-biz additions to the Wimbledon tradition, or the gobs of strawberries and Devonshire cream that were on sale everywhere—I love 'em—but those were just details.

At Wimbledon, everything possible was done for our comfort and convenience. The scheduling of matches, by the legendary tournament referee Colonel Legg, and later his son-in-law, Captain Mike Gibson, was exquisite, when the English weather permitted it. Cars picked us up every morning from our hotels and flats

The die was cast. Margaret Smith was the big Aussie with Centre Court nerves; I was the loosey-goosey kid from the public parks of Long Beach. It was an image that remained for a long time after the reality had changed.

----

all over London and drove us to the grounds of the All England Lawn Tennis and Croquet Club, Wimbledon, about an hour's ride from Big Ben across the Thames and through the traffic maze of south London. There was a Players' Tea Room that was more or less off limits to the press and public. And on and on. The players knew they were being taken care of, and they responded in turn.

Even in the dressing room we were spoiled rotten. The attendant there was Mrs. Robert Twynam, the wife of the head groundskeeper, and she took care of everything, for all of us. We hung our dresses in her drying room at night; she polished our tennis shoes before every match. All we had to do was show up.

And it didn't hurt either that Wimbledon's grass courts were absolutely the best in the world, or that the official name of the tournament was simply "The Lawn Tennis Championships." It would have been very un-British to add ". . . of the World."

Despite all the outward amenities, for me and I think for most players the Wimbledon atmosphere is absolutely filled with tension, from the moment you first drive through the Doherty Gates on opening day until you've either been eliminated or won. Everybody notices the tension in different ways, but for me it all takes place in the dressing room. There are actually three—the lower, middle, and upper. The upper one, which is also known as the Members' Dressing Room, is a large area divided into three cubicles, and off to one end there are four huge bathtubs and a couple of showers, about the best and only place in town to really get away from it all and just be alone with your thoughts. (I'm not normally superstitious, but I've used the same tub after every match I've played there since 1961.) Most of the seeded players are assigned to the upper dressing room by a sort of unofficial caste system. At the start of the Wimbledon Fortnight there are about 25 of us, and we talk and joke around a lot, but even then only to relieve the persistent undercurrent of tension. As the huge field of players is sliced in half, and halved again, and again, fewer and fewer of us show up every day. By the start of the second week there are usually only eight players left. Then four. And then —the last two. By Finals Day the tension is suffocating.

In 1966, the last two were Maria Bueno and myself. We dressed slowly and tried to make small talk, but neither one of us was really up to it. Bueno, a Brazilian with unbelievably fluid, graceful strokes, was always a favorite of the crowds and the press. I was too, back in the early sixties, but not because of the way I hit the ball. *L'Equipe,* the French daily sports paper, said our matches were like duels between the gym teacher and the *professeur de violon*. That didn't bother me too much, but I have to admit I always felt people made too much of Maria's style. Maria was also a very strange sort of person. She was almost aloof. She usually kept to herself, and rarely socialized or even talked with the other players. She wasn't unpopular, but she wasn't popular either. Everybody always seemed to take a neutral attitude toward her, and maybe they were just a little bit wary too.

On that day, though, her personality was about the last thing on my mind. I wanted to win badly. I had never won a major championship, and for the first time I really felt deep down that I could. And if I did, it would mean I'd reached my primary goal in tennis —to become the Number One player in the world. In 1966 Wimbledon was head and shoulders in importance above every other tournament, much, much more than it is now. If you won Wimbledon you practically had to retire the next day not to be called Number One. If you didn't win Wimbledon, nothing else mattered much at all. It was that simple.

I was nervous and edgy, but it was a good kind of nervousness, the kind that comes from anticipation, not fear. I had always played Maria with confidence, even when I lost, and I knew that day I was the better player. All I had to do was prove it.

We finished dressing. We were given the traditional bouquets, one each from both the tournament secretary, Major Mills, and from the referee, Captain Gibson. Next stop—the Waiting Room, located beneath the grandstand of the famous Centre Court just to the left of the entrance onto the court itself. The upper dressing room is on the second floor of the grandstand structure itself. A short walk. We left the dressing room and together we walked past the Members' Enclosure, reserved for initiates of the All England Club and their guests. We walked down a bare hallway, then down a long staircase. On the walls of the staircase were the names of the past Wimbledon champions—Lenglen, Tilden, Moody, Lacoste, Marble, Perry, Connolly, Hoad, Smith, Laver. . . . I didn't look, but I knew that Maria's name was up there too—three times.

Finally we got to the Waiting Room. And there we

waited. No one was allowed in except Maria, myself, and an attendant. Our tennis dresses were checked to make sure they met Wimbledon's rather fussy all-white standards. We knew that Her Royal Highness Princess Marina, the president of the All England club, was in the Royal Box at the south end of the court and we talked about our plans for the ritual curtsey. Not as simple as it sounds. On at least one occasion I'd walked onto Centre Court, curtseyed, and was told later there was nobody there to curtsey to.

But mainly we waited. The room itself was austere, almost barren. There were the traditional fresh flowers, a mirror (I suppose for last-second primping), a hard couch, and two wicker chairs that might have come from a seedy New Orleans hotel lobby. And silence. If it had been earlier in the tournament we could have heard the applause from the matches in progress on Centre Court or the adjoining Number One Court. That day, however, there was only the slight, muffled sound of the late arrivals taking their seats. There was no view of anything. A sadistic place, really.

There was plenty of time to think. I tried to get my head together for the match, but I knew there were over 15,000 people waiting for our entrance and by then I could hardly breathe. I tried not to think about the past, but the memories kept swirling back, as they always have.

I'd always loved Wimbledon, obviously, in a way I'd never loved or even particularly liked a place like Forest Hills. As a kid I dreamed about Wimbledon a lot—daydreams, mostly—and it was always the ultimate. But I was never overwhelmed in those daydreams, I was inspired. I even picked Wimbledon as the topic for a school English essay I wrote in 1958 when I was fourteen, three years before I ever went there. It turned up in some old papers I was going through when I was getting ready to start in on this book.

Thump, thump, thump, beat my heart. This can't be true, here I am in New York City at 5:00 P.M. leaving by plane for Wimbledon, England. I still can't believe it, here I am eighteen years of age and in one week I will be participating in what is considered to be the Tennis Championships of the World. This being my first time to the Championships I was very nervous but I kept telling myself nobody expects me to come out on top but more than anything I wanted to be chosen to the Wightman Cup Team of the United States which is the highest honor in tennis any girl can receive. As I sat there waiting for the time to pass before the plane left, past thoughts kept running through my mind, that first taste of tennis a couple of months before my eleventh birthday, how I saved every cent I had earned for my first tennis racket, that very first sanctioned tennis tournament, I was so nervous I couldn't even hold on to my tennis racket let alone make my body coordinate. As I watched the players of approximately fifteen years of age that first tournament I could not hesitate to think how anyone could possibly obtain this height of play. . . .

In 1957 a man named Joe Bixler who was the Wilson Sporting Goods Representative for Los Angeles and vicinity asked me if I would like to join the Wilson free list. He explained to me that the free list would consist of free rackets, strings, and all the other equipment needed would be wholesale. Here I am still on the free list receiving everything free. Also that first trip East in 1958 when I obtained national ranking of 5th.

Plane for Wimbledon, England, leaving on runway 5. There it was, this is it I told myself, a chance to make my ambition come true. While walking to the plane a handsome young man, with brown hair, blue eyes, and stood somewhat above six feet approached me and asked if I was the young tennis star from Southern California. Nodding my head yes, he introduced himself as Ramsey Earnhart. I asked him if he was going to participate in the Championships also, he said he was going to the Championships but not to play, only to watch. He told me he must leave and remarked he would see me later.

As I came near the plane a familiar sound came to my ears, it was the four engines of the plane roaring. Traveling by plane numerous times it seemed to be the same old routine.

Across the ocean we started. All I could observe was clouds and ocean, the clouds looking like billions of white billowy, fluffy feathers.

After awakening I looked down and I could see that we were decreasing in altitude. Faintly in sight I could see an airport. Just then I remembered that Darlene Hard was to meet me at the airport. She was to drive us to the hotel Hardwick in Wimbledon in her own car. She owned a red '50 Chevy convertible, lowered slightly with twin pipes.

Darlene met me as I reached the bottom steps of the plane. "How was the trip little one," as she always called me. "Fine," I answered.

We got my luggage, then drove to the hotel Hardwick. Darlene had already checked out a room earlier in the day. It was an admirable room with thick, warm rugs and an old-fashioned brick fireplace which was warm in cold weather.

For the next five or six days Darlene and I practiced on the grass courts. Grass is my favorite surface because I prefer the net. Actually we were unable to practice on the courts until 10 o'clock, soonest possible time because of the fog in the early hours of day which England is famous for.

Here it was a couple of days before the Championships were to begin so we decided to rest. Since the Championships last two weeks we knew it would be a strenuous grind if we could last that long in the tournament.

The next day I was introduced to some of Darlene's friends that were living in London. Their name was Mr. and Mrs. Holiday, a typical English couple. They were interested in tennis and knew more about tennis than I had suspected.

We explained to them that we must get home early because the next day was the commencing of the Championships and we would have to awaken early the next morning. They understood perfectly, so we bid them farewell.

The next morning the alarm clock aroused us at 8 o'clock. We decided to have a late breakfast at either 11 or 12.

Becoming Number One

Reading the morning's newspaper to see what they had to say about the Championships, it gave the usual first day overall picture of the tournament, the seedings and the previous record of the favorites. Darlene was number "1" as anticipated and to my surprise I was seeded number 8. My first-round match was to be against Marge Varner of Germany at 3 o'clock. Darlene received a first-round bye.

Darlene took me to the courts about 2:30 and I reported in at the tournament desk. Marge and I were to play on one of the back courts. I played well and was fortunate enough to win 6–1, 6–1.

The next day which was a Tuesday, June 24, 1961, my opponent being Vicki Palmer from the U.S., we played on the number 3 court. It was a very cold, brisk day, with a wind blowing eastward. Even before I could get in the match Vicki was ahead 3–0, then 4–0, then 5–0. I made a furious effort to pull it out but failed at 6–4 in the first. Finally settling down and playing tennis I ran out the next set at 6–1. During the intermission I thought the match over and realized I hadn't been running her forward and backward enough. We then walked slowly to the court and continued the match. I told myself, it's either now or never. My serve was never better and I won the third set 6–2. Whew, was I glad that was over.

In the meantime Darlene was advancing without any difficulty, winning both matches at love.

Next I was up against Shirley Breit, who was a steady, defensive player, so I knew I must keep her running and be aggressive. This was a Friday, June 27, 1961. Today we played on the grandstand court which is the number 2 court, with me the victor 6–0, 6–4. Actually the match was closer than indicated.

Looking at the draw sheet the next day I realized the round of 16's was coming up. This means only 16 players are left in the draw. The tournament committee explained to me that I wouldn't have to play until Monday.

Monday, June 30, 1961, playing on the grandstand court again. As Carol Caldwell and I entered the court, she was the girl I was to play, the King and Queen of England entered the stands so we did the usual curtsey and commenced to play. Carol was the one girl I wanted to beat more than anyone else. It only took me twenty minutes to dispose of her at six games to nil, both sets.

Wednesday, July 2, 1961. Here it was the quarterfinals and who do you think was going to be my opponent, none other than Darlene Hard. To make a long story short she defeated me in three long sets at 10–8 in the third. . . .

So, things like my fantastically detailed daydreams gave me a sense of Wimbledon long before I ever saw the place. When I finally did get there, in 1961, I visited a place that had been a part of me for years. Too much anticipation can sometimes make the reality of something pretty anticlimactic, but if anything, that first Wimbledon was even more perfect than I had imagined it would be.

Karen Hantze and I flew together from Los Angeles. She didn't like England—she had been over the year before and felt it was too old and too inefficient—but I was determined to love the place, and I did. We flew over Ireland, which looked as emerald green as it was supposed to, and then we began our descent into Heathrow. When we broke through the clouds I saw England for the first time—the cars on the wrong side of the streets, the smokestacks everywhere, the tiny rows of houses. Everything looked well-ordered and in miniature. It had been raining on the way in, but the sky was just beginning to clear as we got off the plane and the absolutely first thing I remember was seeing this typical English family—father was wearing a tweed suit, mother wore a sweater and scarf, and all the children had on their little school outfits—and they were all waving handkerchiefs, saying good-byes to other relatives. It was perfect.

We drove to Beckenham, near London, and one of the first people I met was Gerry Williams, the tennis writer for the London *Daily Mail*. We got on right away, had a lot of fun together, and I must have gone on and on about Wimbledon because he finally said, "You've got to see the place before the tournament starts."

I couldn't wait. He drove me out, and when we got near the All England Club he made me close my eyes. Then he parked his car and led me by the hand up through the grandstand until we got to the very top of Centre Court. "You can look now," he said.

It blew my mind, or whatever the 1961 equivalent was. The court was deserted, of course, and there was nobody in the grandstand and hardly anybody anywhere on the club grounds. It was so calm, so peaceful —and absolutely beautiful. Gerry told me Centre Court has seating for 14,000 people and room for maybe another 2,500 standees, but it didn't look that big because it was completely enclosed ("Centre Court" actually refers to both the grass court and the grandstand surrounding it), and there was a roof that extended out to cover maybe three-quarters of the grandstand. It was like a theater, with the one tennis court being the stage. The proportions were perfect. It was a solid, solid place.

Gerry let me wander around the grounds and I felt the atmosphere immediately. It just seeped in. Everything was dark green—the grass, the grandstand, the ivy that climbed all over the grandstand. Just south of Centre Court, across a wide walkway, were the fourteen field courts, neatly bordered by low hedges and separated from one another by other, narrower walkways. And all over were the flower boxes with those pink and blue hydrangeas brought in for the Wimbledon Fortnight. I didn't believe that anything could be so stunning—and inspiring.

I still go out to the All England Club every year to see Wimbledon when it's deserted, just to feel the beauty of the place, and I think of Gerry every time I do. During the tournament itself it's a shame but my pace becomes so crazy that I can't take the time to really enjoy the place in a quiet, relaxed way.

Two weeks later the schedule of matches was posted. I drew Yola Ramirez of Mexico. She was seeded fifth and we were scheduled for the last match of the third day—on Centre Court. It was too much.

Wimbledon usually has good weather. It's almost part of the tradition, so that many English families plan their holidays to coincide with the Wimbledon Fortnight. But 1961 was an exception. It rained off and on for three days, the schedule of matches got farther and farther behind, and Yola and I didn't start playing until very late Wednesday afternoon.

The wait didn't do either of us much good. In the first set I had all the chances in the world but finally lost it, 11–9. Then I began to put everything together, I played well, the sun broke through the clouds and I remember how pretty the black shadows from the grandstand looked on the lush, green grass, and how happy I was just to be there, playing at Wimbledon, and on Centre Court. I won the second set easily, but by then it had gotten dark and the match was put over until Thursday.

God, I was disappointed. I knew if we had kept going I would have won. Yola was in trouble, scared to death of losing to this chubby, unknown kid from Long Beach, California, who was giving her so much trouble.

That night Karen and I bought some ExLax. Don't ask me why. I had never taken the stuff before, but it couldn't hurt, right? Tasted just like chocolate. Well, I misread the directions and I was up all night. In our boarding house—one room with a bed and breakfast for £6 a week—the bathroom was about a mile from the bedroom. By Thursday morning I was absolutely exhausted.

Not that it made much difference. When Yola and I resumed that afternoon, it was obvious she had my

game figured out because in that last set she hit absolutely everything to my forehand. In those days my
forehand was vulnerable, to say the least. I'd kept that
little fact hidden from her the day before but I couldn't
now. I didn't see one backhand the rest of the match
and I lost badly.

That was the beginning of my Wimbledon experience.

The next year, 1962, I again played my first match
on Centre Court, but this time my opponent was a
lanky, awesomely powerful Australian named Margaret
Smith who already that year had won the championships of Australia, Italy, and France and was seeded
No. 1. It was obvious to almost everyone that unless
she fell out of an airplane she was on her way to becoming the next great player in the game. She was tall,
powerful, consistent, and moved beautifully for a person her size—and her game hasn't changed much since
I first met her. Very predictable, very mechanical. No
touch, no finesse, very little versatility. But she didn't
need any of that because she was so damned big and so
damned consistent. She just played the same way every
day and got away with it because she was such a great,
physically imposing athlete. Her personality hasn't
changed much, either. In 1962 she was shy, almost dif-
fident. She trained diligently, liked her tennis, and that
was it—very Australian.

She was getting all the attention then. She deserved
it because of her record, but it was certainly more than
was healthy for her. The pressure on her was unbelievable. She was caught in the middle of a petty
dispute with the Australian LTA and was being ostra-
cized—she wasn't even allowed to practice with the
other Australian women. Nell Hopman, the coach of
the Australian women's team, actually refused to watch
her matches. As an Australian she was adopted by the
English press and English crowds as one of their own.
She was seeded No. 1 and was of course expected to

win the tournament. And she was the star of the Ladies'
Day program (the first Tuesday of Wimbledon is traditionally given over to women's matches exclusively) in
front of a full house on Centre Court. It was a lot to
ask of a nineteen-year-old.

On the other hand, I was a part-time player who
bounced across the ocean every spring to play a few
tournaments and have some fun, then bounced back for
the USLTA grass-court circuit before putting my tennis
racket in mothballs until the following spring. I wasn't
exactly a pushover (I was ranked No. 3 in the United
States for 1961) or an unknown (Karen and I had
won the Wimbledon doubles the year before), but nothing was expected of me at all, and despite all I've said
about wanting to be Number One and all that, I sure
hadn't gotten my head together about it, not at that
point. I was just eighteen and having a ball—I'd even
had a premonition the previous winter about playing
Margaret at Wimbledon and I couldn't wait—and I
loved that Centre Court. I'm not sure Madge did very
much.

Our match was one between two players with a lot
of raw potential but not much else. Neither of us was
a complete player. We weren't court-smart and we really didn't know what was happening. The first set went
quickly and I lost it, 6–1, but I sensed that Margaret's
forehand was getting mushy. She hits it with a very long
backswing, and the wind that day—it was swirling
everywhere inside that Centre Court box—caused her
to lose rhythm and timing. In the second set I jumped
to a 5–0 lead by playing to that weakness and held on
to win the set, 6–3. That evened the match.

The third set was fantastic. Margaret jumped in front
this time, 5–2. At 5–3, on her service, she reached
30–15, two points from victory. But I was unbelievably
loose, and on the next point I broke off a running
backhand passing shot down the line that just stunned

Margaret. I could almost see her slump a little. I broke her service, held mine and broke her again for a 6–5 lead. I got to 40–love, triple match point, on my serve. She put away an overhead. Double match point. I double-faulted, 15,000 people roared, and I could have killed myself. Single match point.

By now the crowd was ready for anything. Word of a Centre Court upset passes quickly through the grounds at Wimbledon, thanks to an electric scoreboard on the outside of the grandstand. Centre Court had been full when we started; now it was jammed—frankly, at the prospect of seeing the top-seeded player lose. The English love upsets.

When I double-faulted, 15,000 people roared, then moaned, then fell deathly silent.

At 40–30 I served to her backhand and came to net. Margaret tried to pass me crosscourt, but I moved in and pushed a backhand volley down the line for a winner.

There was silence, and then a deafening roar of applause.

My first thought was only that I had made it to the third round—honest. (We had both received first-round byes.) I really didn't realize the importance of that match until the next day when the newspapers came out. It was the first time the No. 1 women's seed had been beaten in her first match in the whole history of Wimbledon, and we were headline stuff everywhere.

That was the first time Margaret and I had ever met on a tennis court and I felt—then—we were equal in ability. There's no doubt that during the next three years she was the better player, but at the time of that first meeting there wasn't much difference between us at all—only her position as the No. 1 seed. The press didn't see it that way, though. They wrote about this tremendous upset that had taken place. And they wrote about Margaret's "nerves" for the first of many times, and over the years I think she started to believe the stories herself.

What did they say about me? Just about everything except that I was made of sugar and spice and everything nice. They wrote, ". . . [her game] always suggests a champagne bubble and she takes the whole world into her confidence. . . . Little Miss Moffitt, an ebullient bundle of energy and repartee . . ." and on and on. Now it really embarrasses me to read that kind of stuff.

I eventually lost in the quarter finals to Ann Haydon (she later became Ann Haydon Jones), while Karen Hantze Susman (she had married Rod Susman the previous fall) won the singles, and Karen and I repeated our doubles victory of the year before. But the die was cast. Margaret Smith was the big Aussie with Centre Court nerves; I was the loosey-goosey kid from the public parks of Long Beach. It was an image that would remain long after the reality had changed.

That's the way things stayed at Wimbledon for the next three years, and even later. I was an upset artist and a personality, a chatterbox who talked to herself constantly and had a really great time out there until the time came for me to lose. Which I would also do as pleasantly as possible, then maybe win the doubles and skip town.

People rarely considered my tennis, the fact that my game was really coming together. It was amazing. A couple of years later I'd read reports in the papers of my matches and they all sounded like they had been written in 1962: I had a great volley, shouted "peanut butter" a lot when I missed a crucial shot, slapped my thighs to get myself going, and threw my racket up in the air at the end of every match.

I really didn't mind all that much, I guess. It was nice to have the crowds on my side, and being a minor celebrity (even if it was just for two weeks) was kind of neat, but I really wish that somebody had gotten the message—that my game and my personality were both changing. They were surprised, I think, when I finally did win Wimbledon, and they were downright shocked when I turned out to be a tough, aggressive professional. They shouldn't have been. It was happening right in front of their eyes, but nobody really caught on.

The following year, 1963, I was again unseeded and Margaret Smith was again seeded No. 1, and she played superbly throughout the two weeks. So did I. In the fourth round I defeated Lesley Turner, the No. 2 seed, 4–6, 6–4, 7–5; in the quarters I defeated Maria Bueno, No. 7, 6–2, 7–5; in the semifinals I defeated Ann Jones, 6–4, 6–4. All three wins were considered upsets. Maybe they were to the tournament committee, but not to me. Although I knew I had a long way to go before I became a finished player, I felt I was beginning to move in that direction, and that with the right preparation I was already as good as all but one or two players in the world.

About the finals itself, there just isn't too much to say. I simply wasn't ready. The match was postponed from a Saturday to the following Monday because of rain, and whatever nervous tension I had built up was gone by the time we played. Margaret deserved to win, and she did. But for some reason, that particular loss to Margaret stayed with me for a long time. Literally for years afterwards, whenever I needed something to psych me up before going out to play, I tried to remember the feelings I had during that match, and the sense of utter desolation and failure I felt when we walked off the court. It wasn't a very good feeling and I didn't want to have to repeat it—ever. It was something to avoid, and the best way to avoid it was to win. Just remembering that day got me through a lot of tough matches in the next few years.

In 1964 I reached the semifinals and lost to Smith

again, by the exact same margin that I'd lost to her the year before, 6–3, 6–4. It was an accurate measure of the difference between us. In 1965 Bueno put me out in the semis in three good sets, but by now I was getting frustrated. I was so close to the top that losing in the semis, or even the finals, was the same to me as losing in the first round. Nothing really mattered except winning the whole thing. And by Wimbledon, 1966, I knew it was possible, really possible.

Finals Day that year was warm and windy, and I love to play in the wind. Bueno and I began cautiously. There were three things I wanted to do against her. One, I wanted to serve wide to her forehand to open up the court for my first volley. That worked. Two, I wanted to make sure my returns of service were deep so I could take the net behind them whenever possible. That also worked. Three, I wanted to lob her a lot. In the semifinals against Margaret Smith I had lobbed superbly and Madge was never able to establish any sort of rhythm. Against Bueno this only worked for a while. I won the first set, but in the second she began to feel comfortable with her overhead and began putting away more of my lobs than I would have liked. By the time I caught on, the set was gone—one service break—but I was strangely relieved, like I wanted to get that bad set out of the way and start in on the one that really mattered.

The match had been tense. Maria always played tense anyway, but if she was able to keep her tenseness and lose her nervousness at the same time, she was great. On that day, however, she kept them both the entire match.

I had been tense the entire two weeks, even more than usual. I had played badly the first week, in the early rounds, but during the second week I couldn't miss anything. Still, I couldn't get rid of my tension and relax, and even throughout the last set against Bueno I was very subdued, almost grim, even though it went easily and I lost only one game. It was the anticipation, I think, of finally reaching a goal I had been working toward most of my life. It was coming closer and closer and I didn't want to let anything stop me from reaching it.

On match point I threw my racket in the air and I was suddenly as happy as I'd ever been in my life. Finally, I was Number One. In my mind I was the best player in the world. There aren't any official world rankings; anybody who wants to rank players can, and most tennis publications and their writers can't resist doing so. I was on top of all the lists when they came out a few months later.

Maria and I shook hands at the net and then waited for the presentations. A red carpet was rolled out for Princess Marina from the Royal Box to where the ceremonies were to be held. Maria and I were introduced to the Princess and we both curtseyed again. There was some small talk and then the Princess gave me the silver plate—a salver—that all Wimbledon champions receive.

Then it was over, and time to get on with other things.

5

Breaking into Sports Politics: The Open Tennis Years

ONE DAY during the 1967 National Championships at Forest Hills, I took a little stroll with Bob Kelleher, the president of the USLTA, along the gravel path that leads from the Clubhouse to the Stadium. We bent each other's ears rather forcefully, and near the end of our talk he got down to the nitty-gritty. Politely but in no uncertain terms, Kelleher warned me to cool it in my press conferences or I would probably be suspended by his association. I told him just as forcefully that I really couldn't care about suspensions. "Look at the game, Bob," I said. "I mean tennis just isn't worth a damn and I can't stay quiet about it anymore. Things are so bad I'm not sure I even want to keep playing unless something changes."

How did I get myself into that situation? Well, what I'd done that was so terrible was I'd sounded off in a whole bunch of press meetings about what I felt was wrong with the game. I'd start with a few preliminary remarks about how I felt the members of the U.S. Davis Cup team should not be receiving per diem on a year-round basis and still be called amateurs; about how tennis was still a country club sport whose of-

It was a standing joke that the foreign amateurs couldn't afford to turn pro because they'd have to take a cut in pay. They were raking in $900, $1,000 and from there on up per tournament and used to actually laugh at us Americans.

----

ficials cared more about their five o'clock cocktails and eight o'clock parties than they did about the welfare of the sport. Innocuous stuff. Then I'd come right out in favor of open tennis, aboveboard competition between professionals and amateurs. And I'd finish up by declaring that I, ostensibly an amateur, was already a pro and made my living on the courts, along with just about all of the other "amateurs" I knew.

A couple of days later I won Forest Hills for the first time, and since I'd already successfully defended my Wimbledon championship, that just about assured me that I'd be ranked No. 1 in the world for the second straight year. At my post-match press conference I sounded off again, hitting especially hard on the hypocrisy and shamateurism that had been a part of tennis for years—had supported the system, in fact. Like Queen Victoria, the USLTA was not amused, but I felt I just had to take a stand, and I couldn't think of a better place to do it than at a press conference after I'd just won my own national title.

I'd been aware of the things that were wrong with tennis for a long time, of course, but it had been only in the past year or so that I'd really thought about what new directions the game should take. I also felt that because I was now Number One, people might begin to listen to me. If you're Number One and still complaining, I felt, maybe people will realize that something really is wrong.

What I said to the press at Forest Hills and other places—and to anyone else who would listen—was hardly news to us players or to the administrators. Illegal and unethical under-the-table payments had been made to players for years to ensure their appearance at a tournament, and thus to assure its success. It was something that was bandied about openly in the locker rooms and at those five o'clock cocktail parties, and how much was going to whom was information readily available to anyone who took the trouble to find out.

The system thrived for two reasons. First, from the beginning tennis had been an all-white, country club sport, steeped in the traditions of affluent amateurism that went with such other teatime diversions as cricket, badminton, and polo. In fact, the sport was invented pretty much as a lawn-party amusement, and almost a hundred years later it hadn't changed all that much. The United States Lawn Tennis Association functioned as an organization of rich people—or more precisely, rich people's clubs, the same country clubs, cricket clubs, boating clubs, and tennis clubs where we'd been playing all our tournaments. It was all very simple and logical. The people who could afford to belong to country clubs were the ones who could afford to be amateurs; and, of course, it was these same people who eventually became officials of national organizations such as the USLTA and ultimately of the world governing body, the International Lawn Tennis Federation. And along the way, they remained firm in their resolve to keep tennis traditional and pure—that is, out of the reach of players and promoters who dared to make money by providing the public with good entertainment.

It was a ridiculous idea that they could carry it off forever, because the only true amateur athletes in the history of the world were those people who had money to begin with. Everybody else, I'd say, was a professional, and it made little difference whether he or she were compensated with scholarships, paychecks, or under-the-table expense money.

I don't know. Sometimes I think I'd just like to see the word "amateur" kicked out of the vocabulary of sports, period. Poof. Gone forever. For reasons I don't fully understand, amateur athletes have always been held up as examples of purity and true dedication. I suppose that's because people figure that if these athletes are willing to beat their brains out for nothing, they must love what they're doing. And that's not wrong, actually, but the corollary—that people who earn money playing sports don't love their game and are only interested in the fast buck—just doesn't wash.

I mean, nobody considers an amateur painter, or an amateur writer, or an amateur inventor necessarily more talented or dedicated than a professional. The IRS taxes a gentleman farmer on his profit or loss at the same rate as it does some guy making his living off 2,000 acres of corn in the middle of Iowa. It just doesn't make sense, and yet this amateur ideal has been a revered part of sports, probably since the first Olympics.

Maybe it's because sports, for most people, is a leisure-time activity and they want to make a distinction between their own nine-to-five jobs and their weekend eighteen holes of golf, or whatever. Maybe they figure, why should the professionals get paid a lot of money for something they do just for the fun of it? The answer to that is simple. Because for us it's our work, and with our work we provide them a service—

103

entertainment. I feel strongly that talent ought to be rewarded and services rendered ought to be paid for, not given away.

When tennis players started turning professional in droves, the first thing people said was that we wouldn't play as hard because now we had a guaranteed income. That really burned me up. Does anybody ever say that about a top businessman or a top government official? I'm talking about really the best, because, sure, there are people with big paychecks who goof off in any profession, but not the people at the top, the very top. And that's what we are, the very best handful of tennis players from among the millions of people around the world who play the game.

As far as drive and dedication and love of sport go, I don't think anybody can honestly accuse a professional athlete (the overwhelming majority of us, anyway) of a lack in any of those areas. At its highest level, professional sports—tennis, baseball, soccer, and all the rest—are tough and physically demanding, and none of us would stay with it very long if we didn't enjoy what we were doing.

Before Chris Evert turned professional, I got into a discussion about all of this with a woman who later turned out to be Chrissie's aunt. She said one of the reasons Chris got all that good press in 1971 and 1972 was that she'd turned down the prize money she earned and was legally entitled to—almost $50,000 in 1972 alone—as though that somehow confirmed that her motivation was more pure than the rest of ours. Well, Chrissie's aunt may have been right about the way other people figured Chris, but I sure don't understand that kind of thinking.

Anyhow, I'm getting off the track.

The second reason the traditional tennis system thrived was that the players themselves supported it. I've tried to figure out for years why players never

104

agitated for reform before we started up in the mid-1960s, and the only thing I can come up with is that the best of those players who didn't already have a pile of family money always got paid just enough to keep them happy, to keep them from rocking the boat. Then, if they were good enough, they'd eventually turn professional—and dive to obscurity making those one-night stands the way Pancho Gonzalez, Tony Trabert, Kenny Rosewall, and a bunch of others did. Or else they'd retire from tennis and with great business contacts made through their country club friends, they'd disappear into the obscurity of Wall Street or something of the sort; Dick Savitt, Ham Richardson, and Chuck McKinley, among others, went this route.

Shamateurism worked in many ways, but the procedure was almost always the same. A promoter would call and say, "Billie Jean, we need you for our tournament," and then the negotiations would begin. $300? $400? $500? $600? "Okay, but don't tell anybody else."

$400 a week was super, $600 was all-time; but whatever the figure, it would always be called "expenses." The USLTA allowed a maximum $28 per diem. That came to $196 per week, but since housing was often free (we were put up in private homes) and a hamburger was always my idea of a gourmet meal anyway, I could always skim a few bucks just off that amount, even in an expensive city like New York. The difference between the per diem and the total amount we'd settled on was usually, well, just handed over.

Sometimes there were other arrangements. Like after I got married, a promoter would occasionally offer expenses for Larry and me together, thus doubling the regular per diem. The most ridiculous example of this came in 1966 when Larry was mysteriously entered in the National Clay Court Championships at the Town Club in Milwaukee. Now, Larry's a pretty good weekend player, but even he'd admit he didn't deserve entry into a circuit tournament, let alone a national championship. When we found out what they'd done, we talked a long time about it. He didn't want to play because he'd probably be bumping some deserving junior player from the draw, but on the other hand, it was the recognition of my worth that we'd been striving for, and besides we were in a really bad box financially, so we went ahead. (He lost in the first round.) Expenses, it was always done through expenses, nothing that was actually illegal. Still, it was pretty uncomfortable.

Aside from the per diem, the USLTA held another whip—the overseas tour. For example, a man named Bill Clothier of Philadelphia was heavily involved with the Pennsylvania Grass Court Championships, and he was also the chairman of the USLTA's International Play Committee, the one that decided which players were allowed foreign trips and which weren't. One year he told me he couldn't give me too much money, but if I played his tournament he'd see to it that I could spend a few extra weeks in Europe, or wherever, and really make a bundle. That way he wouldn't have to get his hands too dirty.

We could always make more in a foreign country than we could in the United States—other national associations were even more lax than the USLTA—and foreign players on our circuit, the Europeans, South Americans, and Australians, really cleaned up over here. Especially the Australians, who totally dominated world tennis in those years. It was a standing joke that players like Roy Emerson couldn't afford to turn pro because they'd have to take a pay cut. The foreigners used to actually laugh at us Americans. While we were stuck with our maximum $28 per diem, they were raking in $900, $1,000, and up per tournament, depending on their talent and bargaining power.

Strangely enough, lesser-ranked Americans fared

even better than their higher-ranked compatriots. The American circuit began the week after Wimbledon, and of course the USLTA insisted that all of its top players enter its own major tournaments. But if you weren't ranked among the top five, or maybe the top ten, you didn't have much drawing power, and the USLTA really didn't care where you played. So, for you, it was off to Sweden, or Austria, or Ireland, or wherever for a few gay weeks—at less than the top prices but still a lot more than you could make over here.

Shamateurism. In late 1967, Arthur Ashe, then the No. 2-ranked American, said, "We all deserve Oscars for impersonating amateurs," and he was right on. No question about it.

Actually, for all my heavy talk, I never really made that much myself. In 1967, my last full year as an "amateur," I grossed just under $20,000, but after legitimate travel expenses—air fare, meals, hotels, and the like—my real profit wasn't all that much. After three years of marriage, Larry and I had a bank account of not quite $5,000, hardly a mind-boggling figure, and remember that I was the No. 1 player in the world for most of that time. It was the hypocrisy of the thing that bugged me the most. I wanted the chance to make money, honest money, doing what I did best. It was that simple.

When I criticized the USLTA, I tried to make an important distinction. I wasn't criticizing certain individuals who gave tremendous amounts of time and energy to tennis, I was criticizing the small segment of the USLTA that was involved with running the showcase events in this country—mainly the grass-court circuit, the national championships, and the international team competitions such as Davis Cup, Wightman Cup, and Federation Cup.

I got a lot of help from people on my way up—from

people, but not from the USLTA. Clyde Walker, my first coach, was a perfect example. He would have been there whether the USLTA existed or not, and so would the Long Beach Tennis Patrons, and even Houghton Park. Until events forced its hand in late 1967 and early 1968, the USLTA did very little even to consider tennis in a truly businesslike, professional way.

I'm sure I would have felt differently toward the USLTA if it had ever done anything at all to enhance my personal position by letting me play overseas more, or by giving me more money, or whatever. But it never did. The USLTA paid me $196 a week in expenses —half that if I stayed in private houses—so I could help draw crowds that put money into its pot, and where that money went, your guess is as good as mine. The USLTA always claimed it went for junior development, or to help tennis at the "grass roots" level in other ways, but when I asked to see its budget, it couldn't, or wouldn't, show me.

In 1967 the USLTA was a nonprofit organization run by volunteers. Except for a small office staff in New York, there was no one who made a living from the USLTA, and it had absolutely no commercial interest in the game whatsoever. Because of it, tennis just stagnated for decades, and it took a revolution— a rather mild one when measured against the histories of other pro sports—to move tennis away from shamateurism and the country clubs and into the more legitimate professional arenas.

Well, I never was suspended by the USLTA after that 1967 press conference at Forest Hills, and over the next few months so many other things were going on in tennis that my grievances really didn't mean that much anymore.

Open tennis, when it came, hit the sports world like a bombshell. But even now, just seven years after it finally happened, the tremendous amount of political infighting and bickering that led up to it seems quaintly dated, and I won't bore you with the details. The important facts are these: In October, 1967, the Council (or executive committee) of the British Lawn Tennis Association voted for open tennis; this was the famous October Revolution, the first big blast through the all-amateur wall. In December, the full membership of the British LTA followed suit. And at last, the International Lawn Tennis Federation, after a hastily called meeting in March, 1968, agreed to go along. That was it, although as I've said, it was far from that simple to bring about. And plenty of blood was shed along the way.

The first open tournament, the British Hard Court Championships, began on April 22, at the West Hants Club, Bournemouth. In the first match ever between a professional and an amateur, Fred Stolle, the pro, nervously defeated Peter Curtis, the amateur, 5–7, 6–4, 14–12, 6–1. Ironically, the first professional to lose to an amateur was Pancho Gonzalez, the one player whose magnificent career had perhaps suffered the most by the absence of open competition. He lost in the second round to Mark Cox, 0–6, 6–2, 4–6, 6–3, 6–3. Ken Rosewall defeated Rod Laver for the men's title; and Virginia Wade won the women's title over Winnie Shaw. I couldn't play because of previous commitments. One especially interesting footnote of a kind that was to become increasingly important in the next three years: Ann Jones refused even to enter Bournemouth in protest over the disparity in the men's and women's prize money. Rosewall won $2,400; first place in women's singles paid $720.

Now, the national associations may have been backward, but they weren't stupid. They were reluctant to recognize that they'd blown a hundred chances to make tennis a truly big-time professional sport on their own, but the one thing they feared most from open tennis when it did come was that independent promoters would try to take over the newly professional game. And their instincts were totally correct. By early 1968 there were two groups of touring pros—contract professionals whose loyalties were to their promoters and not to their (former) national associations. One was the Handsome Eight (otherwise known as the Handsome Seven and Tony Roche), headed by Dave Dixon of New Orleans. The other was the National Tennis League, headed by former United States Davis Cup captain George Mac-Call. The NTL had six men and four women under contract. The men were Pancho Gonzalez, Rod Laver, Kenny Rosewall, Andres Gimeno, Fred Stolle, and Roy Emerson. The women were Ann Jones, Françoise Durr, Rosemary Casals—and me.

My negotiations with MacCall didn't take very long at all. I was ready. The winter of 1967–68 I played the Australian circuit for the first time since I'd gone Down Under to take lessons from Mervyn Rose three years earlier. I won four of the five tournaments I entered, including my first and probably last Australian national championship, and I beat Margaret Smith Court (she had just gotten married) in two finals without losing a set. MacCall talked to me seriously for the first time in Melbourne, during the nationals, and it took us about two seconds to come to terms. He wanted three other women for his tour, and his first choices at the time were Margaret, Nancy Richey, and Maria Bueno. Maria and Nancy declined for various reasons, and Margaret said no way unless she got more than I did, which George, from a promoter's point of view, couldn't see giving. I recommended the three women who eventually did sign, and they jumped aboard almost as quickly as I had.

I signed my contract a few weeks later in Los Angeles, and ironically it was negotiated for me by the same Bob Kelleher who had warned me just a few months earlier about speaking out against tennis hypocrisy. It was a two-year deal with $40,000 each year, plus expenses, and I couldn't have been happier. At last I was a professional tennis player, something I'd wanted to be most of my adult life, and for the three weeks between the day our contracts went into effect, April 1, 1968, up to the start of that first open tournament at Bournemouth, the four of us were the only women tennis professionals in the world who actually earned our money by playing.

My last match as an amateur was against Nancy Richey at a special international tournament at Madison Square Garden, and it was one of the most upsetting that I'd ever played. Although one or the other of us had been ranked No. 1 in the United States since 1964, we hadn't played each other for three and a half years, and the last time we had, she'd beaten me in the quarter finals at Forest Hills. I was unbelievably tense. I wanted to beat her so badly I could taste it. We played so rarely that every time we did meet, the importance of the match was blown way out of proportion by both of us.

I won the first set and I got a 5–1 lead in the second. Nancy scrambled through the next two games, but at 5–3, on her service, I finally reached match point. I controlled the point well, hit a solid approach shot that Nancy barely got to, and came to the net. She sent up a weak little lob just barely to my backhand side. Indecision. First I thought I'd play it safe and let it bounce. Then I figured, no, I'll take it as a high backhand volley. Finally I decided to move around it and put the damned thing away with a regular forehand overhead. But by the time I'd finished my mental gymnastics, the ball had dropped too low for me to really do anything with it; I went for it awkwardly—and smashed it about a foot and a half long.

I didn't win another game. Nancy finished off that set

and raced through the third, 6–0. I was just emotionally kaput. I was supposed to be the best player in the world and all that, but boy, I was still pretty immature in a lot of ways. Later, I talked to Laver and Rosewall about the match and they said to just forget it, that you're always going to have a couple of those along the way. But it wasn't very easy to forget, especially since I was turning pro just two days later.

The four of us who assembled in Paris in early April for the start of the National Tennis League's first European tour were amazingly compatible. Not that we had much choice, the way things worked out. Ann Jones was the oldest, twenty-nine, and maybe the brightest. She always understood her opponents very well. She had a lot of guts and was unbelievably tough to play against; I'd say Ann wore me out more often than any other player I've ever faced. She had a good forehand and a vulnerable backhand. She wasn't too aggressive at first, but Laver and Rosewall worked with her on that, and after a few months she really came around and learned to assert herself. Ann and I talked a lot about philosophy and psychology. She was very reasonable about life. She saw it for what it was—crazy.

Frankie Durr was just a delight, a really nice person, and also very bright. Her whole lifestyle was very organized, very precise. She was the kind of person who could tell you exactly where every penny went. I had to work really hard when I played her, because for some reason she'd usually psych herself up more for me than for the others. Frankie was tough—beatable, but tough. She was exceptionally quick and had great anticipation, but I think her unorthodox strokes hurt her. I'd look at her sometimes and just couldn't understand how she could ever hit anything. No serve—none. She should have been born in the United States or Australia instead of France—some place, any place where they teach the right way to serve.

Frankie was twenty-five then and I was twenty-four. Rosie Casals was just nineteen, but she'd already been playing world-class tennis for two years. Rosie was unpredictable, and she had a great, cynical sense of humor. On the court she loved to discover new ways to hit the ball, but she never really worked hard enough on developing the kind of sound, basic game you need to reach the very top. All champions, I think, have one great shot, what I call their bread-and-butter shot, the one they can call on at any time to get them through a crisis. With Rosie, there wasn't any. Very flash on everything, very colorful. But also very erratic—and just not conscientious enough.

When the six men joined us, we began in Southern France. We played Cannes, Nice, Aix-en-Provence—all over—and it was murder. I'm telling you it was bloody murder. The whole tour was nothing but one-night stands, and I was never so tired in my life. Here's what happened every single day: We always seemed to finish playing around 2 A.M., rarely got to sleep until four, then had to get up at six in order to arrive at the airport at seven, or we couldn't get a seat on the plane, which left at eight. We *always* had to catch a plane at eight o'clock. Everywhere. I think every plane in Europe must take off at eight o'clock in the morning. When we got to the next city we'd hop a bus and travel six hours along those meandering European roads, get off the bus, check into a hotel—and within an hour we'd have to be on the court again. That's what we did for almost thirty straight days, and by the end of it I just wouldn't have cared if I died.

We were always laughing because of the stress; there wasn't much else to do. It was unbelievable. In one place the showers didn't work, in another the locker room was covered with cobwebs. The men themselves would sometimes have to lay the portable court we used, and the women would have to help with the taping.

The weirdest place was a little town in Italy, in the Po Valley. We played on an outdoor court, but at night, and the lighting consisted of a few light bulbs strung across the court between some wooden poles. You wouldn't believe the shadows, but that was nothing. The playing surface was brand-new asphalt—it hadn't settled, didn't have any coating, and the balls were so black after five minutes of play that you couldn't see them at all. Even that was nothing, though. Instead of laying the asphalt with plenty of room along the side lines and behind the base lines, this new asphalt—sticking up three inches above ground level—only fit the exact dimensions of the court itself. So when we were behind the base line (to serve, for example) we were three inches below the level of the court, and then when we wanted to rush the net we'd have to take this little hop before we moved in. Nobody foot-faulted, though.

I remember that particular night because, the fact is, I don't remember it at all. It was as though I went to sleep for a set and a half and when I woke up I didn't know where I was. That's when I knew things were getting tense. I do remember thinking, "If this is what being a pro means, who needs it?"

It was a tough life. When we came back to the United States, we had sort of the opposite problem. MacCall couldn't get enough tournaments for us to keep our games sharp. The four of us knew each other's games fantastically well, but any time we'd enter an outside tournament and play anybody we hadn't seen for a few months, we were just up a tree. George was a great guy, but a little bit disorganized. He could motivate anybody to do anything, but he always needed somebody to come along behind him and see to the details, and during those two years there just wasn't anybody around.

He was hilarious. I remember one time he had been promising to take Rosie and me to dinner for weeks, so one night in London (this must have been later, around Wimbledon time) we got a phone call from Paris. It was George. "Meet me at the Guinea for dinner in an hour and a half," he said. Okay. Rosie and I trotted on over and went in. Table for three for Mr. MacCall? Of course, right this way. It was a super restaurant—super food, super prices—and no George. We waited an hour. Two hours. Still no George. By now we were both dying of hunger and we went ahead and ordered. Surely, George would show up any minute. We finished dinner. No George. We finished dessert. No George. And now—panic. No money. Flatsville. We had exactly enough between us to cover the bill without leaving a tip. We sneaked out, mortified.

George ambled in two days later. "Sorry about the other night," he grinned. "You kids have a good time?" It was just impossible to stay angry at the guy.

I was with the National Tennis League for two years. During that time I played the NTL dates and whatever open tournaments MacCall entered us in, which were most of the big ones. As the months went by, however, it was more and more obvious that the NTL wasn't going to make it, and in fact it folded even before my contract was up. By then, most of us were back on the regular tournament circuit full time, only now it was an open tennis circuit.

I guess I'm pretty ambivalent about those two years with the NTL. On the one hand, things were often a mess. But on the other, it gave us women the chance to find out where professional tennis was at that time. It was strange, but from the beginning the four of us were treated almost like outcasts by the other women players. That first year, especially the first six months, some of the other women would hardly talk to us when we showed up at open tournaments. The idea that women

115

could be contract professionals outside the control of their national associations was outrageous, even to many of the other women players. There were a lot of slights —like we wouldn't be invited to a birthday party or something. Small things like that, but they do bug you a little.

In retrospect, though, the two years that the four of us spent on the tour were really our intern years, because when our own tour began in 1971, a lot of the basic things we'd found out about promoting and handling the press and just plain day-to-day existing suddenly came in very handy. The four of us were the ones who were able to guts it out and hold our own circuit together when things got tough.

We learned a lot from the men too. Stolle and Emerson were new pros, but the other four—Gonzalez, Laver, Rosewall, and Gimeno—had been touring pros for years. And Pancho—God, he'd already been at it for almost two decades, since 1949. I saw how they learned to adjust. Gonzalez and Rosewall, the real old-timers, could sleep anywhere—in a car, a bus, an airplane, or a locker room. Not everyone was so relaxed, of course. For example, Stolle, the newcomer, hated to fly and he was so hyper anyway that he wore himself out just sitting down. I learned two things during those years—how to cat-nap and how to drink beer—and I needed them both just to stay alive.

The best times were after the matches when a few of us would go out and try to unwind. The four real veterans would tell us rookies about the really tough days in the 1950s and early 1960s when there was nothing for the pros except what they could scrounge for themselves. For them, the NTL was a luxury. Even though we all knew pro tennis had a long way to go, hearing them talk made me realize it had already come a long, long way.

Pancho especially would tell these stories about how

he would drive alone in his yellow Thunderbird from city to city during the days when he was playing Frank Sedgman, then Tony Trabert, then Lew Hoad and Kenny Rosewall in their head-to-head tours promoted by Jack Kramer in the 1950s, and how he used to pull into the parking lot of whatever high school gymnasium they were playing in that night and fall asleep for an hour or so, then play a match, then grab a hamburger and head off into the night for the next city. It was strange listening to him talk that way because I remembered watching him play Hoad one day in Los Angeles, in 1958 it must have been, and I was so excited I couldn't wait for them to begin. Seeing them play was the big event in my life that year, but for them it was just another one-night stand. And now I was on the other side of the fence. It made me start to realize what the obligations of a professional are. For the player it's often just another match, but for the spectator it's a once-a-year opportunity, and since the spectator's shelling out the bucks, that makes a lot of difference.

As I've said, MacCall was a great motivator. The 1968 Wimbledon championship was the first open Wimbledon in history, and it was very important to all of us that professionals win both the men's and women's singles titles. It was important to George too.

Rod Laver came through and won rather easily, and although I came through too, and won my third straight title, I have to admit I never should have. My knees, which always were trouble, were beginning to go, and the NTL tour had taken its toll and I was exhausted. On top of that, my relationship with the British press and the British crowds, which had been generally fantastic up to then, was slowly but very obviously going on the racks. In retrospect, that entire year was the start of a rather grim period in my life. The years from 1968 to 1970 should have been the best tennis years of my career, but because of a lot of things, they turned out to be the worst.

It's hard for me to explain what happened between me and the British because there are still some things about it that I don't fully understand, but let me try.

By 1968 Wimbledon had become a different tournament for me, and I had become a different person. I still loved Wimbledon, but it was no longer in every respect the place I'd dreamed about and written gushy essays about as a kid. It was becoming, I'm sorry to say, just another tennis tournament. It was still the most important tournament, but with all that was happening in tennis—the new professional tours, the open tournaments, the wads and wads of prize money that were becoming available—it was no longer the only tournament. Not for me anyway.

I had changed too. I was aggressive, I was tough and, I hoped, I was professional. I had long ago stopped being the little chubby prodigy from Long Beach, and as I said before, the British weren't ready for what to them was a sudden personality switch. On top of that, the British love underdogs, and by 1968 I was no longer an underdog. I'd won the thing two years in a row and I'd been ranked No. 1 in the world two years in a row. Now the British were looking for a new face. Which all sounds fine from this vantage point, but at the time I just couldn't handle that kind of new attitude on their part. I felt, plain and simple, rejected. Ever since I'd first started to play tennis I'd always felt that if I ever became Number One I'd be able to share that experience with other people. This became such a part of me that I just assumed it would happen when the time came. And, now that the time had come, and it didn't happen, I was confused and bitter.

All of these things began working together that year, and I could really sense an almost open hostility toward me every time I walked on the court.

As for the press, their animosity toward me had really begun, I think, during the 1966 Wightman Cup matches, which were played that year at Wimbledon a couple of weeks before the championships. The United States was heavily favored, but we fell behind three matches to one—just one more victory by the British and it would be all over. The fifth match was between me and Ann Jones. We split sets and played even in the third to 2–2, 30–all on my serve when I collapsed in agony with cramps in my left leg. If we hadn't needed to win the match I probably would have defaulted, but I didn't, and after a short delay, we contined. I hobbled around enough to win, and we went on from there to take the other two matches as well and retain the Cup.

The next day the press accused me of faking an injury and of being theatrical, and all but said I'd deliberately psyched Ann out of the match. Even Ann's husband, Pip, thinks to this day I cheated her out of a victory that afternoon. It was ridiculous. I know I'm dramatic sometimes, but there's no way I would have tried to pull a psych job like that, especially not against Ann. I couldn't have lived with myself if I had.

On top of all that, I had my knees to think about. The beginning of my knee problems may or may not have started one day in 1963 when I was commuting to college on one of the famous Los Angeles expressways. My little 1950 Ford got caught in heavy traffic and was hit from behind by a bus, thus beginning at least a six-vehicle chain collision. Although I didn't spill any blood, both of my knees struck the dashboard and, as the doctors say, were traumatized.

Athletically speaking, my knees are a gift. For me, personally, they're literally a first-class pain. Like most successful athletes I have excellent lateral movement, and because of my height, or lack of it, I rely on this more than a taller player like Margaret Court does, for

119

example. To oversimplify, my knees swivel more than the average person's; that allows me quick starts not only to the left and right, but also up and back. Which is great. Loose knees, however, are more susceptible to injury than normal knees. Which is not so great. I was once examined by Dr. James Nicholas, the orthopedic surgeon for the New York Jets, who remarked, "Your knees are marvelous, absolutely marvelous. They're just like Joe's." Joe, of course, being the frequently operated upon quarterback of the Jets. Yeah, really marvelous.

In October, 1967, I felt my left knee starting to go. The next spring the pain was much, much worse and I consulted three doctors. The last one said, "Don't worry. When you need an operation, you'll know." But starting right then, I was in almost constant pain for the next three years. Anytime I got into really long matches, or sometimes even just a long rally, my knee would either flat give out or start to burn with pain. I remember especially my semifinal match against Nancy Richey in the 1968 French Open. We got into a fantastic rally on that slow European clay at Roland Garros Stadium and I finally ended it with a sharp forehand down the line that went for a winner. But that one point did me in. My knee just wouldn't work right anymore, and I lost the match in three sets.

I couldn't thrust my leg fast, couldn't get off my starting blocks, and that threw my whole timing off. And it hurt mentally just to know there were certain shots I couldn't get to at all. Within a few months I was taking like six hot baths a day trying to ease the pain. It was the wrong thing to do. I should have been putting ice on it, but I didn't know that.

So Wimbledon that year, 1968, was a joke. I was in lousy shape physically and certainly not in very good mental condition. I won on one leg and sheer deter- mination, and, of course, it didn't hurt to have George

MacCall around to goad me before every match. On top of that, my parents were in the stands—the first time—and I really wanted to win in front of them.

In the semifinals I played Ann Jones and she got ahead one set and 5–3 in the second before I was able to stiffen and hold the line. I won my service at love, and I got the service break by forcing three errors and hitting a backhand winner outright. That evened things at 5–5; then I ran out the set and won the third relatively easily.

In the finals I played Judy Tegart and beat her, 9–7, 7–5. The only emotion I could summon was just a long thanks that the tournament was finally over.

Two months later at Forest Hills I won a drawn-out, three-set semifinal from Maria Bueno, but in the finals against Virginia Wade, no way. I lost quickly, 6–4, 6–2, and two weeks later I had to default in the Pacific Southwest in Los Angeles. That was it. In October I went under the knife of Dr. Donald Larson, my orthopedic surgeon in Long Beach.

In layman's terms, my problem was a mushy kneecap, which not only caused a lack of mobility but also cut off circulation to the calf. The result was cramps. Given my history of leg cramps, I'm a little surprised I didn't need that knee operation long before I finally had it.

Apparently, an athlete's first knee operation is the worst. The problem is not pain, but wondering whether you'll ever be able to play with as much confidence in the knee as before. I'd been warned by Dennis Ralston, who had his own history of knee trouble, that my recovery would be long, and it was. It took six months before I really felt sure about that left knee, but by then my right one was starting to go. Same damn thing.

The next year and a half I'd just as soon forget. There weren't many triumphs and there were a whole lot of disasters. I was fast becoming a cripple again, my attitude was lousy, and my tennis was worse than that.

At Wimbledon in 1969, Rod Laver, on the way to his second Grand Slam, came through for MacCall, as usual, but I didn't. I reached the finals again, but this time I lost to Ann Jones in three sets. If there were hints of a British change of attitude toward me the year before, this time there was no question, at least not in my mind, that they were really down on me. It was Ann's thirteenth Wimbledon, and up to then she'd made it at least as far as the semifinals eight times without ever winning. The crowd was for her, as it should have been. That didn't bother me at all. I love partisan crowds, for me or against me. In Italy, for example, you know immediately where you stand with the crowd. They'll boo you or cheer you or even throw pillows at you, but there's never any doubt about their desires, and it's all out front. But on that day against Ann, I sensed an almost total hypocrisy on the part of the British, something that almost bordered on dishonesty. It was very strange. They'd go through the motions and applaud a good shot of mine, but they did it in such a blatantly cool way that I knew that what they really wanted was for me to dump the ball into the net. It would have been obvious to anyone. I just wanted to scream, "To hell with you. Don't clap if you don't feel that way. I don't care if I'm not your heroine or your favorite. That's fine. She's yours. Just don't give me any of that phony politeness when you don't really mean it."

I hate to say it, but the British fans were just asses that day, everything I'd always thought the British weren't supposed to be. And to top it off, I felt I was getting screwed on the line calls themselves, that the linesmen and lineswomen were making sure Ann won, no matter what.

It had been a lousy two weeks anyway. Larry and I

had argued about something—I don't even remember now about what—and Maureen Connolly had died of cancer just two days before the tournament began. Tennis seemed very insignificant that day, and I was totally broken up by the whole experience.

Forest Hills '69 wasn't any better. I lost to Nancy Richey in the quarters, 6–4, 8–6, although I had a 5–2 lead in the second set. It was an appropriate way to end a miserable year.

By spring, 1970, I was almost positive my right knee would need the same operation my left one had had two years before. There just wasn't any way around it. Surprisingly enough, the last match I played before that second operation was one I've heard some tennis observers think was one of the best Wimbledon finals ever.

This time my opponent was Margaret Court, and measured both by elapsed time and number of games played, our match was the longest women's final in Wimbledon history. It was very well played, I thought, but for me horribly frustrating, mainly because I lost, 14–12, 11–9. And it killed me because I did have Margaret on the ropes—at least backed into her corner—and then let her go. I served for the first set three times in a row, at 6–5, 7–6, and 8–7, but I just couldn't close her out. And when I didn't win that first set I started to play scared. It's true my right knee was bothering me—I couldn't come down hard on it and follow my service to the net—but Margaret was playing on an ankle shot full of Novocaine. So mainly it was just a pressure situation and I blew it. My knee didn't help, but if it had been perfect I might have lost love and love.

I wasted no time. The next week I went under the knife again, but this time there were no problems and I actually almost looked forward to the operation. I knew what to expect, everything went like clockwork, and I was out playing again within two months and even won a couple of tournaments within four—including a big one at Wembley, England.

By then, however, another revolution had hit tennis. This one was for women only.

6

Going It Alone:
The Virginia Slims Years

BY THE time of the 1970 U.S. Open at Forest Hills, open tennis was almost two and a half years old. Very few people had expected the transition from an all-amateur to an all-professional game to go very smoothly. Nobody, however, had been prepared for the new rounds of politicking and the almost daily bickering that took place as the new professionals jockeyed for control with the old-line national associations and the ILTF. It was a mess. How many opens should there be? What was the difference between an amateur, a "player," a registered player, an independent pro, and a teaching pro? (Don't ask.) Should contract pros be allowed to play Davis Cup, Wightman Cup, and Federation Cup? Should pros get expense money anymore, or should they play just for prize money? It went on and on, and people in other professional sports must have looked over at us poor tennis folks and just laughed a lot.

Still, by late 1970, things were beginning to sort themselves out. The men contract pros were now under the single umbrella of World Championship Tennis, run by Texas oilman Lamar Hunt, and WCT was about

Gladys Heldman agreed to talk with Kramer. No luck. "Kramer's an ass," Gladys reported. "First he wouldn't talk to me about it, and then when he did he said he just wouldn't change anything." I was infuriated. We weren't asking for that much.

---

to announce a million-dollar tour for 1971. A rival circuit of so-called independent professionals—those men and women who still swore allegiance to their national associations and to the ILTF—was established, if a bit shakily. And prize money was pouring into the game from all directions.

Only one problem. Very little of it was going to us women.

Tennis was one of the few major spectator sports where men and women had traditionally competed together, although (with the delightful exception of mixed doubles) in different events. Which was fine, as long as the game was for amateurs only. As tennis staggered toward professionalism, however, it became pretty clear that it was a sport controlled by men who were unwilling to even think about giving women a fair shake when it came down to the nitty-gritty—money. Not that we had ever really been considered as equals. Nearly everywhere, except at Wimbledon, women were given second-class treatment. It showed up in everything from court assignments—"Put the broads out there on the field courts somewhere. They won't mind"—to the amounts of under-the-table expense money.

But back when the money was still coming under the table, nobody really cared how much we were getting, especially the men players, because except for me and for one or two others, women weren't getting all that much. And besides, it was every player for himself. But now that things were more or less aboveboard, now that we were actually playing for money instead of just having to show up for it, and people could see how much all of us were (or weren't) making, the cries of anguish were unbelievable. All of a sudden we were considered unfit to play tennis—for money. Stan Smith said women should retire at twenty. (He later recanted, partially.) The Australians, who suddenly became very traditional in such matters, said no way, even some of those who'd been touring pros back in the gloomy '50s and early '60s. I thought there'd be some support from them, at least. But it just didn't happen. Equal prize money for women? Nonsense. Men are stronger and better and they play best-of-five-set matches. Men are the breadwinners, and besides, they're really the ones the folks come to see. Right? About the most support we ever got from any man was from Arthur Ashe, who said, "If the women can go out and make it on their own, fine. More power to them." But then he spoiled it by adding that he didn't think we deserved an equal share when we played in the same tournaments with men.

The disparity in prize money started right with that first open, at Bournemouth, and Ann Jones showed a lot of perception in refusing to play, because in the next couple of years that prize money ratio of roughly 3 to 1 —$2,400 to the men's singles winner, $720 to the women's singles winner—came to look pretty good. In the United States the ratio was 4 to 1, sometimes 5 to 1 (both for first-place money and for the total tourna-

Nancy Moran

Friendly rivals. I beat Chris Evert to win the first Virginia Slims tournament of 1974, in San Francisco; later we teamed up to take the doubles title.

Baby pictures. Here I am in 1944 at the age of one (above) and at three (below).

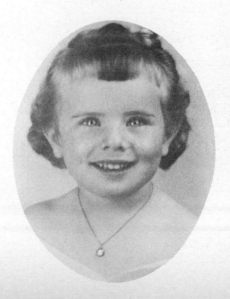

At five showing off my new kid brother, Randy.

Getting into the game.
At 11 with a rather stiff
backhand, and at 12
moving nicely into the
ball.

At 13 talking it over with an early tennis friend, Darlene Hard.

Team Play. Above, the 1959 Southern California Junior Wightman Cup team. From left, Kathy Chabot, Karen Hantze, Carol Caldwell, me, Barbara Browning, Pam Davis. Below, the winning 1961 United States Wightman Cup team. Back row, from left, me, captain Margaret Osborne du Pont, Karen Hantze, co-captain Margaret Varner. Kneeling, from left, Gwyn Thomas and Justina Bricka.

Wimbledon, 1961. Karen Hantze and I leave for England, where we astonished ourselves by winning the Wimbledon doubles title over Margaret Smith (below, far right) and Jan Lehane of Australia.

Le-Roye Productions

Wedding bells. On September 17, 1965, I married Larry King, a cute guy I'd been introduced to three years earlier at Los Angeles State College.

Keystone

Cal. Photo Service

Turning Pro. From left, Anne Jones, Frankie Durr, Rosie Casals and I congratulate Roy Emerson after we'd all signed professional contracts in 1968 with George MacCall's National Tennis League.

Larry and I head home following my 1967 slam of all three Wimbledon titles—singles, doubles, and mixed.

My parents saw me play at Wimbledon for the first time in 1968. Larry was there too, and during the awards ceremony I chatted with Princess Marina.

Linda Penberg

Forest Hills has never been my favorite place, but in 1972,
after I'd won my third United States Open, I felt in the mood
to clown around a little.

RHYTHMS
OF THE
GAME

UPI

Patrick DeLuca

Patrick DeLuca

Patrick DeLuca

Cal. Photo Service

Above, the Moffitts in 1973. My parents, Bill and Betty, and my brother, Randy. Below, the Kings in 1972. With Larry at Forest Hills.

Linda Penberg

UPI

Moments of triumph. In 1971, I celebrated with champagne that day in Phoenix I became the first woman athlete to earn $100,000 in a single season.

Cal. Photo Service

UPI

Two years later, in Houston, I got a trophy and a check for the even greater satisfaction of beating Bobby Riggs.

A GALLERY

OF

OPPONENTS

Nancy Richey Gunter

Cal. Photo Service

Virginia Wade

Cal. Photo Service

Chris Evert

Nancy Moran

Rosie Casals

Evonne Goolagong   D. Berretty/Black Star

Kerry Melville

Cal. Photo Service

Frankie Durr

Having some fun talking up—as usual—one or the other of my favorite causes.

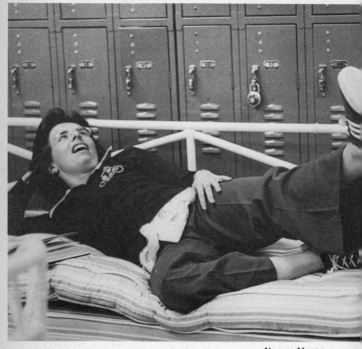

Just goofing off before a match in early 1974.

ment purse). And in Europe it was even worse. In the 1970 Italian nationals I played super tennis and won my first major clay-court championship—and $600. The men's singles winner got $3,500.

At some tournaments—at a lot of tournaments—we didn't get a cent unless we reached the quarter finals, which meant the overwhelming majority of us didn't win anything. And since promoters were now putting all the money they used to give us under the table into the prize-money pot—most of it, at least—in a lot of places we were worse off than we'd been in the good old shamateur days.

At first, my argument wasn't for equal prize money. We couldn't argue that we were as good as the men, or as strong, because we weren't, and in the major tournaments the men did play the best-of-five sets while we played the best-of-three. All that the other women and I agitated for initially was for a better ratio, maybe 5 to 3 or even just 2 to 1.

But even that was unfair to us, because it meant that as entertainers we were still getting short-changed. I began to realize that women should get paid not only for their skill and talent, but because people wanted to watch them play. The best men players were better than the best women, and I'd never said they weren't (although I do wonder what would happen if we played against men on equal terms right from birth; it might be interesting). But from a show-biz standpoint I felt we put on as good a performance as the men—sometimes better—and that that's what people paid to see. Relative strength or how long we spent on the court didn't mean a thing. If our show was as entertaining as the men's, then we should have been getting equal pay. It was really that simple.

The promoters, however, almost all of them men, didn't quite see it that way, and neither did the men players. Whenever a promoter tried to close the gap, which did happen occasionally, the men always screamed that we were taking money from their pockets, and they really resented it.

By the end of 1970, something else was happening too. Slowly but surely the number of tournaments for women was being cut back, because if a promoter didn't have a whole lot of money to pass out—say, no more than $20,000 or $30,000—his inclination was to give it all to the men and have one good purse instead of two small ones. And the fans, he felt, preferred to see the men.

At the time, of course, there was no women's circuit for contract pros, and the contracts the four of us had signed with George MacCall's National Tennis League had expired earlier in the year. So I asked the USLTA what the women's schedule for 1971 looked like. Well, that was quite something, because they didn't have one. Period. Eventually, the ILTF did get around to putting together what it called a Grand Prix circuit, which included most of the major championships of the world. The Grand Prix had thirty-four tournaments for men and nineteen for women. Thanks a lot. So not only were we getting the short end of the prize-money stick, we were getting an even shorter end of the tournament schedule. There were a lot of professional women players by now, but there was little money for us and very few tournaments. We were being shut out. Cold.

All of this came to a head at Forest Hills in September, 1970, when the prize money was posted for the year's last big tournament, the Pacific Southwest Open in Los Angeles two weeks later. First place for the men paid $12,500; total prize money for the women was $7,500, and you had to reach the quarter finals to get a piece of that. I wasn't playing at Forest Hills because of my second knee operation, but I hung around the locker room a lot, and you could hear the screams all the way to California.

"Did you see the prize money for the Southwest?" . . . "Billie Jean, come over here. I want to talk to you." . . . "We're getting left out all the time, more and more." . . . "What are we gonna do?" . . . "We're going no place." That kind of thing. Locker room talk, but angry, really angry.

I can remember first trying to organize women players as early as 1964. That year, as usual, the top foreigners were getting their big fat guarantees—rumors said as high as $2,000 or $3,000—for playing both the National Doubles at Brookline, Massachusetts, and the U.S. Nationals at Forest Hills. But the USLTA gave only that little per diem to the top American women—and to only the top four at that. Nobody else got a dime. Nothing.

I remember Stephanie DeFina and Mary Ann Eisel complaining about that, about having to play in New York for two weeks and not getting a cent, and I agreed it wasn't right. I said, "Why don't all of us get together and agree not to play unless things are changed?" At that time "change" meant more expenses from the USLTA for more women players, and that's all.

Nobody would go along. Nobody wanted to hurt the USLTA and nobody was even ready to defy it. I asked the players what the USLTA was doing for them. "Giving us a headache," they said. I said, "Fine. If you want to run your guts on an empty stomach for two weeks, fine." I was seeded. I was getting my guarantee. If we'd boycotted that year, then I was the one who would have lost the most, but nobody would go along. It wasn't even close. And so I didn't say much after that about organizing things—until 1970.

Now the situation was different. It wasn't just a little per diem dough on the line, it was the livelihoods of a lot of women. Rosie Casals and I went around and talked to nearly everybody. We all agreed that the one person we had to get through to was Jack Kramer, the

131

Southwest promoter. I bailed out of that one, though. Kramer had never been a friend of women's tennis. I knew a meeting between us would be a disaster because he'd think I was just agitating for myself again.

We needed somebody who would represent all the women who were concerned, and we approached Gladys Heldman, the founder, publisher, and editor of *World Tennis* magazine. She agreed to do the dirty work.

Nice of her, but no luck. "Kramer's an ass," Gladys reported. "First he wouldn't talk to me about it, and then when he did he said he just wouldn't change anything."

I was just infuriated. We weren't asking for that much, just a quarter of what the men were getting. But it was no go. (The Pacific Coast Championships, scheduled for Berkeley the week after the Pacific Southwest, actually had the worst ratio ever—$25,000 total prize money for the men and just $2,000 for the women, or 12½ to 1. But *its* tournament director, Barry MacKay, was able to satisfy us by raising an extra $9,000 just three days before the start of that tournament. So it wasn't impossible.)

Rosie and I talked boycott, but for various reasons that was still an impractical move. It was pretty discouraging. Then one day, in the midst of a long and loud discussion in the women's locker room at Forest Hills, Gladys suddenly bounced in and announced she'd arranged an eight-draw tournament in Houston the same week as the Pacific Southwest. She'd made one or two phone calls and just like that had set up a $5,000 tournament at the Houston Racquet Club. She said that bleachers were already being erected and tickets were being sold.

Fantastic. Nine of us agreed to pass up the Southwest—not that there was much to pass up—and play, and a couple of weeks later we showed up in Houston. At this point, the Houston tournament was nothing more than a protest against Jack Kramer and the unfair prize ratio at the Pacific Southwest. It remained for the good old USLTA to kick us out on our own and to simultaneously hang itself. This involves some more tennis politics, but bear with me because it's important.

The USLTA refused to give a sanction to our tournament. (A tournament sanction is permission to hold a tournament. It seems to me that what you get for a sanction is the privilege of paying a sanctioning fee to the USLTA.) First it said it couldn't sanction two major tournaments in the same week (which it had done before). Then it said it couldn't sanction two open tournaments the same week (which it had also done before). Finally, through president Alistair Martin, it threatened to suspend all nine of us.

Then, the week of the tournament, here's what happened:

Tuesday, September 22. The USLTA gave us a sanction for an *amateur* tournament and said it was okay to distribute that $5,000 in expenses, but that we couldn't play for it. That sounded familiar. The USLTA wanted us to go back to the good old under-the-table days.

Gladys announced that she'd had a few conversations with Joseph Cullman, who's a tennis nut. He's also the chairman of the board of Philip Morris and he said his company would sponsor our tournament through Virginia Slims cigarettes. The prize money was jacked to $7,500 and the tournament was given a name —the Virginia Slims Invitational.

Wednesday. Rosie and I argued that we should play for prize money in defiance of the USLTA. Gladys suggested to us that a way around the USLTA would be for us all to turn contract professional, to *World Tennis* magazine, for one week only. If we were contract pros, the USLTA would have no control over us. Eight of us voted right on, and the ninth, Patti Hogan, said she'd boycott future tournaments if the USLTA did suspend us. A contract was drawn up committing us to *World Tennis* for the grand sum of $1 each, and the eight of us signed. A couple of hours later, Julie Heldman, who was laid up with tennis elbow, wandered in and wondered what all the fuss was about. When she heard, she signed on the dotted line too.

That afternoon the tournament began at the Houston Racquet Club. The nine official *World Tennis* magazine contract pros who played were Julie Heldman, Rosie Casals, Val Ziegenfuss, Kristy Pigeon, Nancy Richey, Peaches Bartkowicz, and myself from the United States, and Kerry Melville and Judy Tegart Dalton from Australia.

But it was still just a one-week deal.

Thursday. We Americans were all suspended by the USLTA. Now it wasn't a one-week deal anymore.

Friday. Barry MacKay phoned to say he'd raised that extra $9,000 for his tournament the next week in Berkeley.

Saturday. The nine of us decided to renew our contracts with *World Tennis* through December, 1971, and we all thereby became another $1 richer.

Sunday. Rosie Casals defeated Judy Dalton, 5–7, 6–1, 7–5, to win the first Virginia Slims tournament ever. (I was still hobbed by my second knee operation and had lost to Judy in the first round.)

The following Tuesday, after some more conversations between Gladys Heldman and Joe Cullman, Virginia Slims and *World Tennis* jointly announced an eight-tournament women's professional tennis circuit to begin play the next winter.

The first Virginia Slims circuit tournament was held in San Francisco the first week in January, 1971, and it gave a pretty good indication of how things would work almost everywhere for the next couple of years. Our first problem was to find sixteen women who were willing to defy the USLTA, or other national associations, once and for all. Those of us who'd been suspended in Houston were reinstated a short time later, but we knew now that it might happen again any time. I personally didn't give a damn anymore. I'd had it up to here, and it turned out there were a lot of others who had too. Mary Ann Eisel (by now Mary Ann Eisel Curtis) and Denise Carter came aboard almost immediately, and that gave us seven of the American top ten. Ann Jones and Frankie Durr, of course, were hot from the start, and by the time San Francisco rolled around, Karen Krantzcke of Australia, Darlene Hard of the United States, and Esme Emanuel of South Africa gave us our first full sixteen-draw field. Almost all of us were players who at one time or another had had run-ins with our national associations.

Then came the sponsorship problem. This is oversimplifying, but in brief, Virginia Slims sponsored some of a tournament all of the time and all of a tournament some of the time, but never all of the tournaments all of the time. My husband, Larry, and Dennis Van der Meer, a friend, coach, and business partner, promoted the San Francisco tournament. Their first stop was to see a man named Kjell Qvale of British Motor Cars to ask for the money. Qvale turned the project over to his public relations man, Jerry Diamond. For advice, Diamond called a PR buddy in Los Angeles named Glenn Davis, the former Army all-America football player. Davis called an old buddy of *his* for advice, by the name of Jack Kramer. Unbelievable.

Kramer laughed at Davis, and Davis told Diamond BMC was crazy. But Diamond, bless him, convinced Qvale it was a super idea. We were in business.

From that point I was on a roller coaster and didn't get off for nearly two years. I played some of the best tennis of my life and some of the worst. I achieved a lot, I think, for myself and for the tour, and maybe I failed in a lot of ways too. There were times when I felt that everything was really together, and there were a few times when the pace got so frantic that I felt my mind and my body were just so far out of whack that I knew they'd never get together again. No way.

On that first winter-spring circuit, we eventually played fourteen tournaments in a little over three and a half months, and as the tour expanded, more and more women took a look at the prize money we offered—a minimum of $10,000 per tournament for our sixteen-draw events—and decided to join up. A majority of the women were still reluctant, however. They thought we would fail and they didn't want to risk being a part of that failure, and besides, there was always that rival Grand Prix circuit sanctioned by the ILTF. It was kind of scary. We felt like we were alone, and there were a lot of times when I had my own doubts; but deep down I think I always felt we'd make it—at least that's what I kept telling the others. It's really hard to remember those years clearly now, in part, I guess, because our success since then has probably produced a distorted memory of the way things actually were.

The ringleaders were the four of us who had toured with the National Tennis League two and three years before—Frankie, Rosie, Ann, and myself. In every city we'd hit the media—hard. We'd go to every newspaper and radio and television station in town, and once we got to them, our press was fantastic. But there was always this undercurrent of, "What are you girls really doing out there?" And, "Who's going to want to watch the women play all by themselves?" And, "Do you *really* think you're going to make it?" We got that kind of stuff, a lot of pretty serious skepticism, from the press and from a lot of fans almost everywhere we went.

We often sold our own tickets, and sometimes between matches we circulated among the crowds and talked with the spectators—Frankie, with her appealing

French accent and her great smile, was especially good at this. We tried different scoring systems, like "No-Ad," to cut short those long, dull matches that seemed to go on forever. We paid the officials—not much, just a token, really—but enough to let them know they were expected to perform professionally. We tried to cut down on the ridiculous number of officials for each match (there can be as many as thirteen), and once later on we even tried dressing them up in those black and white striped shirts that basketball referees wear, to make them look like real officials instead of pall-bearers. We tried anything that we thought would make our tournament fun for the spectators—without interfering with the seriousness of the tennis itself—anything at all to get rid of that stuffy, tedious atmosphere most of us felt had always surrounded tennis tournaments.

If my life had been fast-paced before, starting that winter it began to resemble something right out of *Future Shock*. It was that way for all of us—everything very mobile, transient, temporary. To have said that I had a permanent address would have been a joke. It was a constant succession of hotels and motels—no more being put up in private homes. I ate out all the time, mostly junk food, and I think I must have averaged three hours' sleep a night the entire three and a half months. Larry had his schedule and I had mine, and even on those rare occasions when we found ourselves in the same city we'd just as likely wind up in different hotels simply because our daily schedules never coincided.

I began to think that maybe things weren't forever anymore—ideas, places, and even friendships. Especially friendships. The days were gone—at least I felt they were for me—when you grew up and lived in the same place, maybe even in the same house, for fifty years, and got to know people really well. If I got to see somebody for a concentrated period of, say, a week, though, it was hard to realize that I might not see that person again for another year, or maybe ever again. Arthur Ashe used to say, "It's tough always having to say good-bye," and now I was really finding out what he meant.

But the tour came first, and everything had to be exactly right. When it wasn't, I admit I got pretty impatient. My friends said I was too intense. They told me to take it easy, that in life you were allowed some fun and games, at least once in a while. I just couldn't relax, though. Practically overnight, we women were trying to change a tennis structure that had existed for a hundred years, and when things didn't happen as fast as I felt they should, I had to know why. If there wasn't a good crowd someplace, I had to find out if the promoter had really been doing his job. If the press coverage was lousy, I got curious about whether the public relations person was on the ball. I wanted my interviews to be just right too. I didn't like to give them "in my sleep"—reciting the same answers to the same old questions time after time—but sometimes I had to. The questions got to be pretty stale and I sometimes wished the press would do a little more homework, but I tried to appreciate that most of them were asking their questions for the first time and I wanted my answers to be just as spontaneous and enthusiastic the tenth time around as they'd been the first.

I played great tennis that winter, especially considering that I was doing public relations stuff almost all the time that I wasn't either practicing or actually playing. My second knee operation had been just beautiful, and I was playing without pain for the first time in over three years. I couldn't miss. I beat Rosie in the finals of the first four tournaments we played, in San Francisco, Long Beach, Milwaukee, and Oklahoma City, and the fifth week I beat Ann Jones in the finals in Chat-

tanooga and won a coonskin cap in addition to my
$2,500. When I lost to Frankie Durr in the Philadel-
phia Indoors the week after that, it was the first time
I'd been beaten since that first Virginia Slims tournament in Houston almost five months earlier.

I played in thirteen of the fourteen Virginia Slims
tournaments that first winter season and I won eight of
them. I also won $37,000 in prize money and I was
beginning to get the idea that I could become the first
woman athlete ever to earn $100,000 in one year. I
knew that would be nice for me, and I also felt it
would be super publicity for our tour.

The one sour note was my abortion. I'll talk about it
more later on, but for now, let me just say that I got
pregnant in late February, skipped a tournament in
Puerto Rico a month later so I could fly home to
California and have the operation, and three days later
foolishly showed up in St. Petersburg, Florida, to play
in a tournament called the Virginia Slims Masters.

I felt fine for the first couple of rounds, but in the
second set of the semifinals I began to dehydrate and I
had to default—to a sixteen-year-old Florida schoolgirl
named Chris Evert. It was the first time we'd ever
played, and that one match, I think, made a tremendous
difference in our later relationship on the court. It
helped establish her as a new personality on the American tennis scene (although she had a lot of other good
wins that year too) and set up our rather dramatic
meeting in the semifinals at Forest Hills five months
later.

That first tour was a success, although a mighty
shaky one, and I didn't come to feel we'd reached the
turning point until the beginning of the summer-fall
tour in August. We played in Houston again, this time
at the Hofheinz Pavilion. During the winter the crowds
had never been super and even here we didn't sell out.
I don't know for sure what it was, but for the first time

I got a really strong feeling that the fans and the players both were very enthusiastic about what was going on. Maybe it was the money—we played for $40,000, the biggest purse so far—or maybe it was just the fact that we were in the city where the whole thing had begun, but whatever it was, I think our whole collective frame of mind changed that week. Things always seemed better after that.

1971 was a good year for tennis phenoms. At almost exactly the same time Chris Evert started to show her stuff in the United States, another teenager, Evonne Goolagong of Australia, was doing her thing on the pre-Wimbledon European circuit. In fact, she won the French Open in early June, an amazing accomplishment considering she'd never even played there before; getting used to that slow clay surface at Roland Garros just might be one of the hardest things for a non-European to do in tennis.

Although Evonne had played in Europe the year before, her record hadn't been all that impressive and I never really took much note of her. Now, however, things were different, and by the time we all got to Wimbledon I couldn't help but notice that Evonne was getting the same kind of treatment I'd gotten there almost ten years earlier. She was the new darling of the Centre Court crowds and she was just perfect for them —shy, self-effacing, very schoolgirlish—and she had a great game. Potentially she was by far the best of the younger players. She had a superb backhand—she could hit either a topspin or a slice with equal effectiveness, which is very rare. And she covered court beautifully; a very fluid player.

But Evonne did have her weaknesses. Her forehand was a little dicey and she had no second serve at all. More important than all of the technical things, however, was her attitude. On match point or at other key times in a match, she was tough. At other times, though, not so tough. She was mentally lazy, I felt. She could come off with the most unbelievable shots, just slam something off the tips of her toes, and then turn around and miss the easiest shot in the book.

I was seeded No. 2, behind Margaret Court, and Evonne was No. 3, and the two of us played in the semifinals. It was supposed to be *the* match of the championships—the new kid on the block against the old pro—and I wanted to be ready. I'd skipped part of the European season to rest up for Wimbledon and I'd gotten through the early rounds in pretty good shape, but in that semifinal I came up flat—nothing. And I had absolutely no excuses.

We played even the entire match. Evonne was alternately brilliant and pedestrian, and although I played well enough technically against her, I was just mentally *blah* the whole time. I kept waiting for something to inspire me. I felt that if I ever got going I could break the match wide open. But I never did, and I lost, 6–4, 6–4. Mentally, I guess, I was in neutral the whole afternoon, and after the match I was just totally depressed.

At Forest Hills, though, in the U.S. Open, I made sure the same thing didn't happen again. This time Chris Evert was the showpiece, and rightfully so. She'd had a stunning year. She hadn't lost a singles match in almost seven months against most of the best players in the world, and she was being touted as the greatest thing to come along in American tennis since Maureen Connolly won her first American title in 1951 just before her seventeenth birthday.

Tournament Director Billy Talbert and Referee Vic Seixas scheduled Chris's first match ever at Forest Hills for the Stadium, and she responded by beating Edda Buding, 6–1, 6–0. Then she beat Mary Ann Eisel —again in the Stadium—4–6, 7–6, 6–1, saving six match points along the way, and it was that one match

141

that made Chrissie a star. The fans loved her, and her next two opponents didn't stand a chance. Both Frankie Durr and Lesley Hunt were absolutely petrified before they even walked on the court—the Stadium court, of course—and lost three-setters. Poor Frankie was in tears at the end of her match. She'd simply never played before that large a partisan crowd before -and she couldn't handle it.

I was delighted that Chris was bringing out the fans and really turning on the people in New York, but a lot of the other women players weren't. They liked her well enough personally, but they were jealous that she was getting all the attention. They felt she was capitalizing on the publicity women's tennis had gotten all during that year without doing all that much herself in the way of promotion, and they even resented me a little bit because I didn't agree with them.

We played in the semifinals. I'd come through my quarter of the draw without too much trouble, but I admit I was beginning to wonder if Chris wasn't destined to win this tournament the same way Evonne apparently had been to win Wimbledon. I have to say, the pressure got to me. I felt it was one of those few matches in my career where literally everything was on the line—my personal standing and the future of the Virginia Slims tour. I felt that if I wound up the year with losses to both Evonne and Chris in major championships I really might be finished as a world-class player, and since neither of them had played the Slims circuit up till then, I knew that if Chris beat me it might knock our circuit right out of the ballpark. How could we claim we had the best talent and that our circuit was the future of women's tennis if our best player—me— was going around getting knocked off left and right by a couple of teenagers?

It was almost too much for me. After I warmed up on a field court I went back to the dressing room and took a shower—and right there with that warm water streaming down on me I guess my nerves just took over, and I started to cry. I stood there and bawled my head off. It was *bad*. For a few minutes I really panicked. I wanted to run, to do anything at all except walk on that court and play that match.

But finally I said, "My God, you've got to get a hold of yourself, Billie Jean. It can't end here, not now."

This may seem like it was a pretty melodramatic moment, but, believe me, it was a very real one. Just like in all those stories, my life tumbled in front of me—my dreams and my hopes for women's tennis and everything else—and I was determined not to let this moment get beyond me, out of control.

By the time Chris and I walked into the stadium, I was back together again, and there was no way I was going to suffer the same letdown I'd had at Wimbledon. The contrast with Evert must have been startling. She had already been nicknamed "The Little Icewoman" and she didn't miss a beat. She was calm and poised. I, on the other hand, was as psyched up as I'd ever been in my life. I talked to myself and slapped my thighs just like in the good old days—except this time there wasn't anything bubbly or effervescent about me at all. I was taut, but I was tough as nails too. It was a grim, professional afternoon. I knew exactly what I wanted to do and how to do it.

The crowd roared when she came back from 0–40 on her service to win the first game. I didn't let that bother me. I shut them out completely, because I knew how I was going to play her and I was confident my game plan would work. I gave her a lot of variety and I changed my depth, my pace, and my spins on almost every shot to keep her from getting control.

In the seventh game of the first set it finally paid off. Chris double-faulted for 0–15, and after a long back-court rally I broke off a perfect dropshot for 0–30.

Those two points decided the match. I went on to break her service in that game and ran out the set, 6–3.

Chris was finished. I didn't let up at all in the second set and it was over quickly, 6–2. It was really strange, but when the match turned in my favor, so did the crowd. I was proud of myself that day, and I think that for one of the few times in my career I was able to really communicate to an audience what it feels like to play great tennis under the most difficult circumstances imaginable.

Four days later, after a lot of rain had postponed the finals twice, I beat Rosie Casals in straight sets for the title—the second United States championship of my career. It was a super tournament, one of my best ever. I felt just terrific afterwards. I felt I had accomplished a lot.

Two weeks later my roller coaster took another nose dive, this time in the finals of the Pacific Southwest. Again, Rosie was my opponent. The match started routinely enough. We played to 6–6 in the first set. Nothing unusual about that, except one particular lineswoman on a base line had given both of us about six or seven lousy calls, and it was beginning to get to both of us, especially me.

On the third point of the tie-breaker, Rosie ended a long backcourt rally by hitting a ball over the base line. Out. Not by much, but clearly out. The lineswoman, the same one who'd already blown a half-dozen calls, missed on this one too. It was a crucial point and I turned and said, "You've got to be kidding."

Then I very calmly went to the umpire and said, "Please remove that lineswoman."

He wouldn't make a decision.

Rosie walked up and I asked her how she felt.

She shrugged her shoulders—she's much more casual

about those things than I am—and said, "Fine with me, Old Lady. That woman's out to lunch."

I told the umpire, "You have the power to remove her and I have the right to request her removal."

The umpire said, "That will embarrass her."

I then asked for the tournament referee, who just happened to be Jack Kramer. In a few minutes another official, John Coman, came up and said Kramer couldn't be found. Kramer, I knew, was up in the television broadcasting booth, on the air, but he could have made himself available if he'd wanted to.

By now the crowd was getting edgy because they didn't have a clue as to what was going on. After a long discussion, both Coman and the umpire finally agreed to remove the lineswoman. Fine. I walked back on the court—and she was still there.

Now I was getting edgy. I'd been pretty calm up to now, but this was too much. And still no Kramer—the one man who, according to the rules, should make a decision. One of the things I'd been fighting for all year was to increase tennis professionalism, and that included the officiating. I wasn't upset because the lineswoman was still there so much as I was because Kramer refused to come onto the court and function as the tournament referee. He was still up in the broadcasting booth.

"That's it," I said. "I'm not playing." Rosie and I picked up our rackets and walked off the court. Double default.

The reaction was predictable. Jim Murray of the Los Angeles *Times* was just one of many who really blasted me. He began a column, "Billie Jean Moffitt King has never forgiven Nature for the dirty trick it played on her in preventing her from being free safety for the Green Bay Packers . . ." and went downhill from there to conclude, "When she walked off the court . . . in a sulk over some inept calls by an unpaid lineswoman, she showed that, no matter how much she gets paid, she's still an amateur."

Maybe. I agree now that it was a bush thing for me to do. What Rosie and I should have done was simply stay on the court and refuse to play until Kramer either came down out of that booth and personally made a decision on the lineswoman, or defaulted us himself. But it seemed at the time that I just had to make another stand. Fans and players expect good officials in a pro basketball game, for example, and they're mightily upset when they don't get them, and I don't see any reason why tennis—professional tennis—should be any different. I think Kramer was pretty bush too.

Then the roller coaster turned up again. The next month I won a Slims tournament in Phoenix and went over that $100,000 mark in prize money, and that put the icing on a great year. I'd won nineteen of thirty tournaments and dominated the Virginia Slims circuit, and as a surprise little bauble I'd played in enough of the ILTF Grand Prix tournaments to pick up that title too. But when the various world rankings came out for 1971, Evonne Goolagong was No. 1 and I was No. 2. I was happy for Evonne—after all, she'd won two major championships in the space of a month—but I was disappointed because it meant a lot of people, including the ones who did the rankings, didn't really give full credit to the Slims tour. I felt that being able to play good tennis week in and week out ought to mean as much as winning major titles. Maybe more, even. But a lot of people didn't see it that way.

I feel that 1971 was my best year ever in tennis. Nearly everybody else feels 1972 was. Whoever's right, I just know one thing. I'd like to forget the first two months of 1972 ever happened. Erase it completely. Gone.

It started out fine. The Virginia Slims winter-spring

circuit cranked up again in San Francisco in early January, and I started out just like I had the year before —with a win. I beat Nancy Gunter in the quarters, Virginia Wade in the semis, and in the finals Kerry Melville and I played a super match which I won in two tie-break sets, 7–6, 7–6. Great, I thought, just like '71. Nothing to it.

I didn't win another tournament for two months.

In Long Beach, Frankie Durr killed me, 6–3, 6–0, and that was my home town. I skipped a tournament in Hingham, Massachusetts. In Ft. Lauderdale, Chris Evert bombed me in the finals, 6–1, 6–0, and it obviously wasn't even close. Two weeks later in Oklahoma City, Betty Stove put me out in the quarter finals, 6–3, 7–6. All of them, I felt, were bad losses, not just because I'd been beaten, but because I was playing horrible tennis. I didn't quite understand what was going on, but I had a pretty good idea.

First of all, I was finding out fast there's a limit to how much tennis—good tennis—I could play in a year. All the other professionals, both men and women, were too. The pro tours had created a great opportunity for all of us, to win money and destroy our bodies at the same time. In the good old days we could get by picking and choosing our tournaments, and there was always room to take time off, but now there was something going every week. Basketball, football, and baseball players all had seasons that lasted anywhere from six to eight months, but we tennis players were going year-round. And the better we were, of course, the more matches we played. Rod Laver wrecked his back and wrist, Tony Roche destroyed his elbow, John Newcombe tore up his knee, and Billie Jean King seemed to be just plain wearing out.

Second of all, even though the Slims tour was in its second year, it wasn't yet well enough established so that any of us could get off the practice-play-promote merry-go-round. Especially me. All I really wanted to do was play good tennis, but 1972 was the year I really became a celebrity, I guess, and if anything, the demands on my time for interviews, television shows, and just plain old public relations were even worse than they'd been the year before. Which was good for the tour, I suppose, but it sure didn't do me any good on the tennis court.

I was also finding out a lot about people and how I related to them, and some of the things I discovered weren't very pleasant. This really happened all through 1971 and 1972, but it bothered me the most right at the start of that second year.

My image—what other people thought I was like— was horrible. People I'd never met, of course, only got to form an opinion of me through television, when I'd usually be in a charged-up setting of some sort, or by reading about me in the newspapers. And I must have had a really bad reputation, because when I'd meet some of these people for the first time in a small group —or better yet, one-on-one—they'd first stare at me as though they expected me to be rough, mean, and musclebound to boot. They'd say things like, "You're not Billie Jean King. You can't be." It was kind of fun showing them I wasn't really an ogre, but I gotta say it wasn't so much fun to know I was considered one in the first place.

I was getting lonely, too, just because I'd have to protect myself against the nosiness and downright rudeness of total strangers, and what I was quickly coming to believe was their seriously misplaced idolatry. People I'd never met before would say, "Can I do something for you?" But what I felt they really wanted was to be a part of me, or touch me, or somehow identify with me. I sort of understood that, but I just hated it.

I remember that one day while I was having breakfast in a coffee shop somewhere, this guy I barely knew casually pulled up a chair and sat down without even saying, "Hello," or, "May I join you?" And I was really ticked, because the one thing I dislike the most, I guess, is lack of respect for my privacy, and this kind of thing was starting to happen everywhere. I'd been told that Wilt Chamberlain never eats out in public when he's on the road. It's always room service. Now, Chamberlain would stand out in any crowd, but I was beginning to sympathize with his problem totally.

I could respect a person's sincerity, and if I sensed that, I'd give him or her all the time I could; but I started objecting when I found out that all a lot of people did was indulge in hero worship. That indicated an imbalance to me, a certain lack of priorities. Maybe I felt so strongly about this because I'd only asked for three autographs in my life. When I was a teenager, Clyde Walker once took me to the Pacific Southwest and I got Pancho Gonzalez, Lew Hoad, and Tony Trabert to sign that little piece of paper—and I had my picture taken with Tony—but the only reason I even did that was because Mr. Walker suggested it, and frankly it didn't mean that much to me even then.

I don't understand that reflected glory bit, and certainly not the groupie mentality, the kind of thinking that makes a young girl say, "I think Joe Namath's neat. I'd love to go to bed with him." My God, she doesn't even *know* Namath. Never met the guy. I remember the first year Tony Roche made it big in tennis there were girls swarming all over him, and he was so shy, so shy. I said to him once, "You're a star now, baby. You're in big trouble."

"It's great trouble," he said. "Right?"

I don't know. I'm not so sure.

Whatever turns you on, but I thought the important thing was to appreciate talent, not idolize it. Like the Rolling Stones. I appreciated their music, but I certainly didn't want to go to bed with Mick Jagger. Times were changing, though. By then the Virginia Slims circuit even had its own groupies, the fellows who hung around our tournaments.

This whole thing really started to bug me, and when that happens long enough, you either get burned out or you change. I found I was doing a little of both. I was wearing out and I was also becoming more isolated and more distrustful. As I said when I was talking about Wimbledon, I had always felt that when I became Number One I'd be able to communicate with more people and maybe have a fuller life—and in some ways I had—but I was also finding out that the very fact I was Number One (in my mind, anyway; forget those 1971 rankings) had put up a barrier between me and other people that none of us could break down. As a tennis player, I wanted to be separate from them, to be the best, but off the court I wanted to be accepted on my own terms as a person, just the way I was, without any frills. But it just wasn't happening. To me, I was Billie Jean King. Period. To them I was a star, and there was no communication.

Even on the tour, I felt there was a distance between me and some of the other players—most of them, in fact. Some of that I could understand. Although we women on the circuit worked together, traveled together, and helped each other with mundane things like picking up plane tickets and making hotel reservations, the camaraderie was largely artificial. Tennis is a very individual sport, and in the end you win or lose by yourself, and you laugh or cry by yourself, too. There aren't any teammates around to share with or lean on.

That was okay. What I didn't like was the jealousy and envy I felt coming from the other players. I could maybe understand them not being too crazy about my tournament wins or my $100,000, but they were also resentful of my publicity, of the fact that I was the one who always got asked to talk to the press and make the public appearances. They didn't realize that first of all I would have been more than happy for them to share the load, and second of all, whatever publicity I got meant the tour was getting it, too. And the tour meant them.

In fact, I wasn't even sure I knew what the word "friend" meant anymore because I was constantly having to try to redefine friendship in terms of what I'm talking about now. I didn't feel that I really had any close, intimate friends. I felt close to two women, Tam O'Shaughnessy and Wendy Appleby, but they were qualifiers and I rarely got to see them. I felt the one person I could trust was Kristien Kemmer, but even that fell through. I'd known Kristien a long time and she'd come to me for advice on everything from tennis to personal matters for years, and I'd gone to her for advice too, but one day she just popped up and said it was over, that her goal was to be Number One and we just couldn't spend a lot of time together anymore. That's pretty grim.

By the time we got to Washington, D.C., in late February, I'd just about had it. All of these things were coming to a head. I was wallowing in self-pity, and my tennis was lousy. And to top everything off, that abortion of mine suddenly made the news (in a pretty big way, as you'll see). I was at absolute rock-bottom and I'd never been so confused in my life. When I suffered my rather predictable loss, Larry and I bailed out for Hawaii immediately and I really didn't know for several days whether I'd ever come back to competitive tennis again.

In Hawaii, Larry got me to jog a mile or two a day, which I hate to do even when I'm feeling good, but I didn't play any tennis at all for ten days except for some social doubles. I skipped the next Virginia Slims tournament, and we went back to Berkeley the Monday after that.

BILLIE JEAN

I had to be in Dallas the next day if I was going to play in the tournament scheduled for that week, the Maureen Connolly Brinker International, a memorial tournament to "Little Mo" that was now a part of the circuit. I didn't know what to do. I had no energy, no pizzazz. I just bounced back and forth mentally between being happy for the tour's success and feeling sorry for myself because I couldn't handle the personal pressures anymore.

When Larry and I got home that Monday, I asked him to hit with me, just for a few minutes, at a court not too far from our apartment. As we played, I kept going from one extreme to the other. "I'm going to retire." . . . "I'm going to play." . . . "No, I'm quitting for good." . . . "I'm playing. I've got to play." This went on for about five minutes or so and I finally just walked up to the net—I remember that I was very tired and very sad—and I said, "Larry, I can't play Dallas. Call them up and tell them I'm not coming."

"Okay, hon," he said. "If that's the way you feel. Are you sure that's what you want?"

"Yeah, I'm sure. It's all over."

And so I retired.

On the way back to our apartment we had to walk through two huge parking lots and I'm still not sure what happened, but by the time we got home, I'd changed my mind—again. Just reversed myself completely.

"Don't call Dallas," I said. "I can't cop out anymore. I'm gonna play. I'm gonna be sore and I don't care if I lose in the first round, or to Evert or Goolagong or whoever's there, but I've got to turn myself around, and Dallas is gonna be the start. That's it. Finished. End of discussion." And I hopped the next plane to Texas.

I still think the draw there maybe was rigged a little bit, because I was only seeded fifth and I drew Chris in the quarter finals. Many writers felt before the match that because of what had happened in Washington, if I lost to Evert now I would quit, for real. Not true—not at that point. The match was important, but only because it was the first step toward my real goal—to win back my Wimbledon title.

Chris and I played even to 6–all in the first set and then to 4–4 in the nine-point tie-breaker, and then I pushed an easy backhand volley six inches wide to give her the set. I trailed badly in the second, and every muscle in my body hurt, I was so out of shape. But then I just dug in. I wasn't going to lose if it took forever, and it almost did. I finally pulled it out at 7–5 in the third, and the other players said it was maybe the best match they'd ever seen on the tour. I don't know about that and I certainly didn't care then. I defeated Goolagong in a three-set semifinal and I lost to Nancy Richey Gunter in two sets in the finals, and I didn't care about those matches either. I just knew I was back from wherever it was I'd been, and I felt everything would be okay the rest of the year.

It was better than okay. It was super. It took me about four weeks to get back in shape, but then I went on a real tear and didn't lose another match for over three months. I won some circuit tournaments, then went to Europe and won my first French Open, a couple of small English tournaments, and at Wimbledon I avenged my loss to Evonne the year before by defeating her in the finals, 6–3, 6–3. Then, after a so-so summer, I again got back into gear and at Forest Hills successfully defended the U.S. Open title I'd won the year before without losing a set.

By the end of the season I'd won another $100,000 and even that ILTF Grand Prix championship again, and this time there was no doubt about the rankings. I was No. 1 again on everybody's list for the first time since 1968, and I couldn't have felt better.

I was even detecting a change in attitude toward me

by the other women on the tour. Earlier in the year Mona Schallau and I had driven together from San Francisco to Los Angeles for some reason, and she'd really been down on me, about all the usual things. "Billie Jean, you're completely overpaid," she said. "The tour's fine and I'm glad I've got this opportunity and all that, because if I play well I know I'll do all right, but you top players are just getting too much money."

I gave her the usual answer. "Look," I said, "from a promotional standpoint, having our top player make $100,000 is great. People look at that magic number and they can see the whole tour's for real, and when they think like that it helps everybody down the line because they're going to want to come out and see us play. If I, or whoever is Number One, was only making peanuts, nobody would care."

We talked about a lot of other tour problems on that trip, but when we got to Los Angeles she was still convinced I was making too much money.

Well, a good bit later, at the last tournament of the year—Boca Raton—Mona and I were talking again. "Billie," Mona said, "forget everything I said that time in the car. After seeing you, or whoever's Number One, go through all the kinds of hassles you've been going through, I guess you deserve every cent you can get. Maybe you don't even make enough."

I was a little taken aback, but I was delighted to hear her say that. It was a perfect way to end the year.

7

Time for a Breather:
Stinson Beach, Fall, 1972

THE LAST few months of 1972 had been super on the tennis court. I was Number One again, and by now I felt confident that the Virginia Slims circuit, although it still suffered from growing pains, was definitely established as a real force in tennis. I was really delighted about both these things.

But the pace had taken its toll and by the end of the year I was washed out physically and emotionally drained. Except for an occasional enforced break now and then—like that week in Hawaii—my life for the past two years had been an endless succession of not only tennis but also public appearances, airport lobbies, interviews, motels, meetings, and dirty laundry. I'd set my goals and I'd reached most of them, but I didn't feel that I'd ever had any real peace of mind. I couldn't honestly remember the last time I'd felt relaxed, and I was just starting to realize how hard and fast I'd gone during that time. It was all like a dream, and to this day I don't really believe I went through what I did.

The circuit always got stronger, but it never reached the point where one of its top players could take a week off, and the demands on my time as the ringleader and

When Arthur Ashe cried in the middle of the Stadium, I didn't like what I saw because it hurt me to see him suffer like that, but the fact is he was revealing the truth of what any competition is all about.

Number One player were absurd. Interviews after our matches until two o'clock in the morning . . . talk shows at six o'clock the next morning . . . personal appearances . . . "Just a few minutes more, Billie Jean." New York City was the worst, but it was like that everywhere, and there were times when I really didn't know what I was doing, when it was all just foggy and hazy and I didn't even know what I was saying. Talk about giving interviews in my sleep, I almost *did* a couple of times. I lived and breathed tennis because I wanted to see the circuit go and I was delighted when I could see it progress. But finally I just turned into a robot. Times away from the Slims circuit weren't much better either, because even at places like Wimbledon and Forest Hills, writers and other people wanted to know what we were up to, and I felt an obligation to tell them as best I could.

When I think about what I did during those two years, the only thing I come up with is "Tennis, interviews, promotion; tennis, interviews, promotion," and I can't get beyond that. I remember asking myself at the time, "Haven't you done anything else at all, Billie

Jean—anything?" And my answer was, "No, baby. That's *all* you've done. You won nineteen tournaments out of thirty one year, and twelve out of twenty-seven the next, and you did so and so many TV shows, and you gave so many interviews, and that was all you did. Nothing but a bunch of numbers."

There must have been some other things, a few good times along the way—there had to have been—but if there were, I couldn't remember them. I couldn't cut through the fog. I was successful, reasonably well off financially, ranked No. 1 in the world—and I was just numb.

So, after that tournament at Boca Raton, Florida, in mid-October, I flew back to California and just took off. For three solid months.

It was the first real rest I'd allowed myself since I'd started playing tennis full time in 1966. The time off for my knee operations I didn't feel counted because of the anxiety involved, and it seemed like the only other times off were also spent in or near a hospital for one reason or another—wisdom teeth, tendinitis, and little things like that. It was the first chance in years I'd had to really reflect on things and to try and see them a little more clearly. It gave my mind time to catch up with my body—once I got used to not having a schedule. *Future Shock* says that people who live nomadic lifestyles are the trend-setters, which is fine with me, but it also says that when we're not on a super-tight, frantic schedule we tend to go bananas because we don't know what to do with ourselves. That's exactly what was happening with me. For the first two or three weeks back in California, I'd wake up every morning with a start and wonder, "Geez, where am I supposed to be today?" And then it would hit me—no place at all—and I'd rack out again for a few more hours. In time it got to be pretty great.

I really enjoyed being able to stay up late and not

have my days planned by other people or outside events. I read a lot, or I did a lot of nothing, or I got in my car, turned on the stereo, and just drove.

Mainly, I went to Stinson Beach, which is the name of a little town and a state park north of San Francisco on the ocean side of Marin County. To get there you follow California Highway 1 up a little way through some hills as you cross the peninsula, and then you drive along the ocean until you come to a corner where there's a restaurant and a dirt road going off to the left. The restaurant is where I'd go sometimes on the way to the beach, just a little local jive place run by a family, with a bar at one end, a serving counter at the other, and about three or four tables in between. You follow the dirt road past some funky little wooden houses for awhile, and then you turn left again and drive down almost to the beach.

I'd always go to the same place. There was a stump at this one particular spot—a tree trunk, actually—that I could lean up against and just look out over the ocean. Up to the right was Bolinas Bay, and down to the left were some hill cliffs, and that was that. I'd just sit there, maybe write some letters. Or I'd just think. I was resting my body, but I was resting my mind too, just trying to get it uncluttered. I tried to reflect on the past year—my whole life, really. I tried to sort things out, and I tried to recapture those things, those events that had made me happy in the past. I looked at clouds, and I remembered that as a child I used to wonder what trees thought about, and fish, and birds, especially seagulls.

Those three months weren't a turning point. That would be a little too dramatic. I don't want to imply that I went there on the edge of a breakdown and received a vision of the future or anything like that. Or even that I spent ninety straight days sitting against a tree trunk looking out at the ocean. I did some business, went to Los Angeles for a couple of weeks, saw a lot of movies, and generally did the kinds of things most everybody does. But that was sort of the whole point—I could do normal things again, and I could shut out the rest of the world anytime I wanted to. It was my call for a change. No telephones, no appointments, no tennis—cancel everything.

It was a real transition period for me, however. Those three months gave me a chance to sum up a lot of things, to try to put in perspective everything that had happened to me in the past, and think some about why it had. What I really wanted to do, I think, was to find out what I was, maybe, even who I'd been in the past and what I'd be like in the future. If somebody asked, I guess I wanted to be able to describe myself.

The big question for the last two years, of course, and even before that, was why I'd allowed myself to be hassled in the first place. Simple. Because I wanted it. After all, no one ever held a gun to my head, even—especially—during those 2 A.M. interviews and 6 A.M. talk shows. No one ever forced me to help promote the circuit, or to play in tournaments when I would have been better off on a beach somewhere like I was now, not really.

I came up with two basic answers, and the first was that I had a pretty healthy ego and it needed to be massaged almost daily. Every athlete has an ego, at least every good one, and, I suppose, so does anybody else who voluntarily puts herself or himself on public display. How else could we walk out onto Centre Court in front of 15,000 people and do our thing? Every time I played a match in front of a crowd—anywhere—I was in effect saying that people were watching me play because I had something to share with them—my talent. And what they gave me in return was applause and recognition. An ego boost.

I'd always played for other people, and I'd always had a very good sense of crowds, maybe like an actress's almost. Even if I went to some really small tournament and found that the people in the stands, or the promoters, or anything at all about the place turned me on, I'd decide right then and there that I'd try to play great tennis. Not just because I wanted to play well —although that was always a part of it—but because I wanted to give pleasure to others. And I felt that the better I got, the more that this kind of thing would happen, that when I reached the top I'd really be able to explain what it was like to be Number One, and that they'd love me even more for it.

But it didn't work out that way. Instead, I found out that the crowds, and the press especially, always had a preconceived idea of what I was like, and that preconception usually came from remembering what I'd been like years and years before I became Number One. I wasn't the same person anymore—who doesn't change a lot over a period of, say, ten years?—yet the fans and press wanted me to be the same person I'd been when they first met me.

That was the conflict: what I was versus what other people wanted me to be, and there were times when I was resentful and bitter when I found out they weren't willing to accept me the way I was.

Maybe I can explain this in another way. When performers sense this conflict, it's very easy for them to stop being themselves, to start playing to the audience entirely, to act the way they feel the crowds want them to act so they'll still get that applause and ego boost. For a tennis player, this can be really dangerous, sometimes fatal.

At Wimbledon in 1972 Evonne Goolagong got caught up in this conflict. As I've said before, Wimbledon loves its underdogs, and their sweetheart was this ideal loser—Little Miss Dunkirk belovedly going down

7–5 in the third. That year Evonne was still very young and inexperienced, even though she'd won the title the year before, and I felt then she'd always be what the crowds wanted her to be. They'd even given her an excuse for losing—her "walkabouts"—the same way they'd given Margaret Smith Court her "Centre Court nerves" ten years earlier. And God forbid she should ever assert herself as a tough, competitive athlete the way I had.

In the semifinals that year Evonne played Chris Evert. I watched the match on television from the dressing room and I could see that Evonne had her mind on the grandstands, not on the court. Every now and then she'd eke out this feeble grin like she was thinking, "Oh, yeah, I'd better smile now." She got behind a set and 0–3 in the second, but I suddenly noticed a change in her during the next game. I thought to myself, "If she wins this game, she'll win the match." She did win the next game—the next six, as a matter of fact—and did win the match, because she stopped trying to please the crowd and got on with the business of winning.

But if that didn't remind me of myself at her age! I wanted everybody to love Billie Jean King and I just knew that when I became the champion they'd love me even more. No way.

I felt like that about the outside things connected with the Slims tour too. But it seemed that the more public relations I did and the more interviews I gave to promote the tour, the more jealousy and envy I got from the other players, and it upset me. Even when I kept on winning tournaments.

I think I'm being honest when I say I'd always been able to enjoy the success of others. I could be happy for somebody like Evert or Goolagong when she won a tournament, even at my expense; and even after that miserable Wimbledon experience in 1969 (I keep using examples from Wimbledon because things seem so

magnified and intense there) when I lost that bitter
finals to Ann Jones, I think I felt happy for her even
though I was crushed myself. I would like that feeling
to be reciprocated by others in similar situations. I remember a press conference of Virginia Wade's after I'd
beaten her at Wimbledon one year, when she said she
really was the better player that day and that I'd only
won because I was lucky. Now, I sure didn't expect
Virginia to be crazy about the fact she'd lost, but I
wonder, why couldn't she have been just a little bit
happy for me?

Rosie Casals was another perfect example. She had
often told me that she wanted to become Number One
while Margaret Court and I were playing because that
would mean she'd reached the top against the very best
players of her generation. Right on. I respected her for
that, but I think she envied my position so much that
she learned to hate me. She tried not to, but I really
felt sometimes that what she was thinking was, "I want
what you've got so badly that I've got to find a way to
somehow destroy you." It was just amazing. It bothered
me—more than just bothered me—and I didn't understand it at all. Was I expecting too much of other people? Maybe so.

So, my ego was the first thing that was causing a lot
of my hassles. The other was the fact that I was a perfectionist, both off the court and on it. Problem was,
perfection is something that happens very rarely in tennis and hardly at all anywhere else. But that didn't stop
me from trying. I was very intense about everything I
did. If I didn't win a point just exactly the way I
wanted to, if the ball didn't skim the net and land two
inches from the line, I'd really get upset. And off the
court I was the same way. I'd bowled maybe twenty-
five times in my entire life, yet every time I went up
to that line I expected to knock all the pins down. Even

at parties, when everybody would be drinking and goofing around, I'd make jokes and laugh harder than anyone else around. It was the same intense thing. Larry felt I had a curse on me because I was a perfectionist, and maybe he was right.

None of this would have been a problem, of course, if I'd been just another player on the tour, a nice, unobtrusive quarter-finalist or semifinalist who maybe sneaked in and won a tournament every now and then, and I sometimes envied the women in that position. But being Number One was a twenty-four-hour job, and my personality just didn't allow me the luxury of letting up at all, even for a minute. I would just as soon collapse first, and I came close.

I guess I'd always been that way, but I sure didn't know why, any more than I knew why I had good lateral movement. The compulsion to succeed was just something that was always there, like my loose knees, my 20/400 eyes, or my craving for ice cream. It was original equipment. I couldn't stand not to be heavily involved in something I was a part of. Maybe it would have been easier if I'd been something besides a tennis player. I doubt it. But anyway, I was a tennis player, and there was so much to be done to try and change the sport, I felt, that the pressures just kept building and building. And too often when I took a stand on something, I felt I was misunderstood. People tried to attribute motives to me that just didn't exist, and the kind of talk that got back to me was, "Oh, Billie Jean? She's trying to be radical, as usual, and she's just popping off her mouth again."

An example of this involved the 1972 Wightman Cup matches. For years I'd played on the Wightman Cup and Federation Cup teams, enthusiastically at first, more grudgingly later on—but I always played.

In the amateur days, things were okay, but by 1972

nearly all the top players were professionals. (About the only important exception was Chris Evert, who couldn't accept prize money because she wasn't eighteen yet—another nonsense rule that eventually got changed, too.) That year the USLTA offered the Wightman Cup players a token fee of $1,000 each—not much for one of the major sports events in the world. I didn't feel the money was right and I was fed up with Wightman Cup politics, which had been a mess for years, and so I refused to play.

The money really wasn't important, but the principle involved was, because it tied in perfectly with what I was trying to accomplish for women's tennis—to make it more professional and it seemed a good issue to fight over. Well, immediately the rumors started. The first was that I'd refused to play because I wasn't offered enough money. True to a point, but not the whole story. The second was that I would have played if the USLTA had made me the playing captain. Not true at all. I was, in fact, offered the captaincy—indirectly— but I just didn't believe in playing captains. That one, I understand, was started by the USLTA itself.

I wound up being an unpatriotic ogre—"How can you refuse to play for your country?"—just because nobody bothered to listen when I was talking about my real motives. It was not a matter of whether or not I would play for my country; I just wouldn't play for the USLTA.

This kind of thing went on constantly. The pressures from inside me and the pressures from the outside kept building and building, and I knew that by the end of 1972 I'd have to do something about them because it was inevitable that similar things would come up the next year, or the year after that, or the year after *that*. I couldn't do a whole lot to change my personality, but I felt that maybe I could at least try and control things a little better, and pick and choose my hassles with a little discretion.

But how?

Sometime in the spring of 1972—I can't remember exactly when or where it happened—Vicki Berner, who was still playing the circuit then, rushed up to me with a copy of *Atlas Shrugged* and said, "You've got to read this. You're Dagny Taggart. You're just like her."

In the next few months I read the book and thought about it a lot, and during those days out by the tree stump at Stinson Beach I realized that Vicki had been exactly right; that in a lot of ways I really was like Dagny Taggart. That one book told me a lot about why I was the way I was, and why other people reacted to me, sometimes pretty strongly, the way they did. It's impossible to summarize the book in a paragraph or two, but it seemed to me that the two main themes of the book, how an intense love for something can be a source of both strength and weakness, and how success can sometimes breed envy, jealousy, resentment, and even hate, were right on the mark.

It made me see how my love of tennis and what I guess you might call my fanatical desire to see the women's circuit make a go of it worked both ways. It kept me going when I'd maybe rather have been taking a week off or at least getting a good eight hours' sleep, but it also made me vulnerable to criticism. If I hadn't really cared about what I was doing, then people could have said anything they wanted about me and it would have just rolled off my back. No sweat. But I did care, a lot, and that's why I didn't understand and couldn't accept all the bad feedback I was getting. I had the guilts sometimes because I wasn't strong enough to realize that I was doing the right thing. Instead, I found myself thinking, "Maybe I'm not right about this or that after all." And the confusion was making me learn to hate something I really did love.

I decided, over a long period of time, to become selfish. That's an awkward word, because all my life I'd been taught to be altruistic, to give unto others and all that. But what is altruism? It comes down to the old question: Is the philanthropist who gives ten million to some charity acting out of true altruism or out of self-interest? Had I gotten involved in all those hassles just "for the good for the game" or because that's really what gave *me,* Billie Jean King, the most pleasure and satisfaction? The answer, of course, was both—it wasn't a question of either-or—but understanding that I didn't have to feel guilty about my motives, despite what other people said, made things a whole lot easier for me.

I knew that what I was doing was helping tennis (although I think I'll leave it to others to judge exactly how much), and I felt that I didn't have to worry much anymore about whether I was acting out of a pure desire to help or self-interest. It just didn't matter anymore.

This revelation, if that's what it was, was already having some beneficial side effects by the end of 1972. It became very easy for me to ignore tennis fans, for one. If they were for me, fine; if they were against me, that was fine too. I simply got on with my playing and didn't worry about them.

I found I was able to stop having to justify the money I made. People said I was becoming mercenary, and that used to bother me. But why? Money sure wasn't the end of the rainbow and I'd never felt it was my only motive for playing, but I also felt that I earned everything I made, and that I deserved what I got. And it hadn't come easy, either. I'd worked my fanny off for every cent.

I decided I was responsible to myself first, and to no one else. If I wanted to do other things besides play tennis—make public appearances, give interviews or whatever—I would, but only because *I* wanted to, and not anybody else.

I remembered maybe the one really good time I'd had during those past two years. The tour was in New York City—this was in March, 1971—and we were playing in an absolutely miserable armory at the corner of 33rd Street and Park Avenue. Nothing was going right. The crowds were lousy because most people didn't even know where the tournament was, and even if they found the place they couldn't be sure what was going on inside because it looked like a jail or a fortress or something. The lighting was terrible, I was playing badly, and I'd just found out for sure I was pregnant. It wasn't a very jolly week, but after my last match I just took off and around 2 A.M. went over to the Vanderbilt Athletic Club in Grand Central Station and gave a clinic for some of the ball boys and ball girls—boom, just like that—for no better reason than that a couple of very dear friends had asked me to.

I had a ball. Kids are fun to work with anyway because they really appreciate the help you're trying to give them, and it was a very upbeat yet low-keyed evening—or rather, early morning. It was a marvelous experience, but the point of it was that I'd done it as much for me as for the kids or the two people who'd asked me to come over. That night was for me more than anybody, really, and it was the only time something even close to that happened from then on until I skipped off to Stinson Beach. And I was determined to make a lot more time for that sort of thing in the future.

I also took a pretty close look at how I acted on the court—my behavior was sometimes pretty volatile and it was always emotional—and I decided I didn't have much apologizing to do about that either. I'd always been emotional—I'm a very up-and-down person—but

that had always been considered bad by most traditional tennis people. What they wanted was a nice,
quiet, phlegmatic sort like Chris Evert, Stan Smith,
or the Australians—all the Australians. They wanted
everybody to be a Rock of Gibraltar, and when a
player like me or like Ilie Nastase came along, they
didn't know what to do. I'd always been taught to be
a lady, which was fine as far as it went. But who was
kidding whom? That's not the way it was out there, not
at all. Players were straining their guts out because tennis is a tough, competitive sport, and if you don't believe that you ought to wander into a locker room
sometime during a tournament and just see the range of
emotions. Sometimes when I'd hear that polite little
clapping that goes on at most tournaments I'd want to
just scream, "You people have no idea what we're
going through out here." Why hide the fact that tennis
is emotional? When Arthur Ashe cried in the middle of
the Stadium at Forest Hills after losing to Nastase in
the finals of the U.S. Open in 1972, he was showing
his true emotions. I didn't like what I saw because it
hurt me to see him suffer like that, but he was revealing
the truth of what any competition is all about.

I knew I liked playing on emotion and I didn't see
any reason to hide it any longer. I would try to be calm
when I sensed an explosion was coming, but I discovered that was worse than flying off the handle for a
little while, because then it would all start to bottle up
inside and pretty soon I'd find myself not even caring
whether I won or lost. It was just part of my makeup
to want to let loose, and so why not?

I don't mean to imply that I suddenly decided to become a bad sport, because I don't think I did. But I
did stop worrying about whether my court conduct was
okay from somebody else's point of view. And that
goes right back to what I said earlier about playing for
myself instead of others.

One thing that was happening at the same time everywhere in sports, I think, was that we athletes were stepping off our little pedestals all over the place. We didn't necessarily conform anymore to the Middle American, middle-class ideal of the athlete who never drank, never smoked, never played around, and was always nice to kids and ate hot dogs. Which was great, because the image of the ideal athlete had always been just that—an image. Many athletes lead exemplary lives, but many don't, either, at least not the kind that sports merchandisers and public relations types want the public to believe we lead.

But the public isn't dumb. People are kind of glad to find out their heroes are real human beings, after all, even if they don't approve of everything we do. Maybe the change started with the publication of *Ball Four* by Jim Bouton. I don't really know, but whatever happened, a new kind of sports hero started to emerge. People learned that maybe Bobby Fischer was a fanatic, Joe Namath ran around a lot, and Mark Spitz was a money-grubber, and they loved it. At least part of the time. And so did I.

I wasn't necessarily in favor of fanaticism, running around, or money-grubbing, but at the same time I was delighted that we were finally being recognized as people with real emotions and desires and not as gods and goddesses who came down off Olympus every now and then for a few hours of fun and games. It indicated to me that there was a new honesty about sports personalities, and I was happy to be a part of that.

Just as an aside, however, this new honesty has presented one interesting problem in tennis, and I really don't know the answer to it. The problem is this:

According to traditional etiquette, you're always supposed to say at the end of a match that you never played better, whether you won or lost. The implication is that if you won, your opponent simply caught you when you were hot and the defeat really wasn't as bad as the score indicated. Or, if you lost, well, you gave it all you had and your opponent was definitely the better player. Okay?

Now, among the Australians especially there's a sort of unofficial code which says: If you're injured, don't play; and if you play, you're not injured. Still with me?

Well, at Forest Hills in 1972 Rod Laver was upset by Cliff Richey in the fourth round and it just killed me because my expectations are always so high for Rod. I really felt bad for him, and as it turned out, he was dying inside. He'd hurt his back in an earlier match and he could hardly move. He practically had to be undressed in the locker room afterward.

Should he have said anything?

I don't know. I really don't. If it had been me, and if I was hurting as much as Rod obviously was, I think I would have simply chosen not to play. And I wouldn't have played for sure if I felt there was a chance of permanent injury.

By the end of my Stinson Beach vacation I felt I'd begun to enter a third stage in my development as a tennis player, not so much in terms of goals and achievements as in how I reacted to people and events around me. The first stage had begun when I made that first trip to England in 1961 and it had ended in 1966 when I took the plunge and decided to really play tennis full time. I was young, innocent, and pretty naïve, and although I think I sensed the problems that faced tennis—anybody with even the smallest vision could see the hypocrisy, incompetence, and unprofessionalism that were hurting the sport—I really didn't know what I could do about them. In fact, I wasn't sure that I wanted to do anything. I was the darling of Centre Court, the upset artist, and I loved it all. Although I made a few waves, I was really only a small source of irritation to the people in the USLTA and the ILTF,

171

like maybe an annoying rash, and I'm sure they felt I'd eventually go away with a little scratching. Or at least do what practically every other female athlete in their experience had done—retire and raise a family.

The second period, from 1966 right up through most of 1972, was a crazy mixture of great success on the court and sometimes bitter disappointment everywhere else. It's really true that it's harder to stay on top than it is to get there, and I discovered many times, first as a player and later as an agitator, that success not only breeds contempt, but also, on occasion, envy, misunderstanding, and jealousy. For me, the results were the loss of friendships and trust, and an almost total, devastating loss of whatever idealism I might have had before. But near the end of that period there was also a time when I finally started getting things together, really together, from the inside, and the fact that I could do that made all the struggles worthwhile.

Now, I felt, I was ready to begin a third stage, one where everything that I'd learned about myself and other people would let me put all of the hassles and conflicts I'd been through into some kind of perspective. I didn't think the hassles would just disappear or anything as nice as all that, but I felt confident that I could cope with them better than I ever had before and maybe direct my energies more firmly than I had in the past. I felt I was more mature, and that I'd laid a pretty solid groundwork for whatever might happen in the future.

About the same time, I began writing this book—for two reasons. The first was because I guess I just wanted to; the second was because a lot of people said they were interested in my life. That seemed good enough for me, but over the next few months I realized that I was becoming more than just a successful athlete, or even a successful woman athlete, and that now people wanted my views on everything, not just women's tennis.

Next question: "What right do you have to be a spokeswoman and go around making all of these pronouncements? In the end, aren't you really just only a tennis player?"

That's a legitimate question and a difficult one. The only real answer I can give is that because of my prominence, or notoriety, or whatever you want to call it, I've got a platform. I'm in a position to be heard out. There are certainly a lot of women who are more intelligent than I am and better informed about things like Women's Liberation, for example, but they can't reach anybody. What I have and what they don't have, simply, is a forum. I certainly don't make any great claims for myself, but if people are willing to listen to "Billie Jean King, woman tennis star," and if what I say strikes a responsive chord, then I feel that's justification enough for speaking out.

Besides, I'm not just a tennis player anymore.

8

Thinking Things Through: Lifestyles, Women's Lib and All the Rest

WHEN the Women's Liberation Movement began to make a big splash in the late 1960s, my first reaction to it was pretty negative, I've got to admit. I thought it was a collection of fanatical, bra-burning women who hated men, and I really didn't have too much use for it. I'd never considered myself particularly radical about anything, burning bras was definitely out, and as far as men went, well, I sure didn't hate them and in a lot of ways I preferred their company. The men I knew usually had some kind of athletic background, or at least an interest in sports, and I found they generally had a better understanding of what I was all about than most women did. I was a little uneasy around women, especially those who weren't into a career the way I was. I didn't disapprove of women being wives and mothers, not at all, but that kind of life seemed to require the kind of social small talk and small outlook I just wasn't comfortable with. Although tennis was one of the few sports where men and women coexisted reasonably well, it was still a man's world, and I found it was pretty hard for me not to be caught up in that. Even several years later, after my thinking about Women's Lib had

The implication was clear. There was Margaret who'd given up tennis so she could have a baby, and there I was in a real depression because I'd done something I'd feel guilty about the rest of my life.

----

changed a lot, I remember standing up to give a speech to a practically all-women Lib audience and blurting out, "I'm sorry, but if you guys were all sportswriters I'd feel a lot more comfortable." The women broke up, because I think they understood what it had been like for me all those years to be in a profession dominated by men.

Women's Lib is a pretty personal thing in the end, I think. It's fine to talk about the history of the Movement and discuss Lib theory, and for the one or two percent of the women who can do that, great. But I know for a fact that the Movement has gotten hung up a lot of times on trivia in the interest of radical purity. Sometimes I think Libbers don't want to move three feet forward if they have to slide an inch to the side at the same time. *Ms.* magazine, I understand, once turned down a year's worth of advertising and a neat five-figure deal from Virginia Slims because it didn't like the slogan "You've Come a Long Way, Baby." That's ridiculous. Virginia Slims was supporting women's tennis, which was certainly part of the Movement, so why lose all that good dough that could be used to spread the word? Libbers get down on me because I sometimes say "girls" instead of "women." Big deal. I sometimes say "boys" instead of "men," too. I occasionally feel the movement wants to create a new stereotype of the liberated woman almost as much as it wants to rid women of the old stereotypes. And one stereotype is just as false as the other.

When it comes to Women's Lib, I'm pretty much of a pragmatist, and I'd bet that most other women are too. Maybe you start comparing paychecks and find you're not making as much as the guy sitting next to you who's doing the same work. Or you apply to med school and find out you're going to be the only woman in a class of 200. Or you want to keep in shape when you're in college and learn there isn't any women's intramural sports program but that the university has just contracted for a $3.5 million basketball arena. Little things like that. Pretty soon you start thinking, "If I'm getting a lousy deal in my little world, I wonder what's going on with women in other places?" So you check around and find your experience isn't unique in the least. Then you decide to do something about it and all of a sudden you're part of the Movement. That's pretty much what happened with me.

To me, Women's Liberation means that every woman ought to be able to pursue whatever career or personal lifestyle she chooses as a full and equal member of society without fear of sexual discrimination. That's a pretty basic and simple statement, but, golly, it sure is hard sometimes to get people to accept it. And because of the way other people think, it's even harder to reach the point in your own life where you can live by it.

It's impossible for me to separate my tennis career from my personal life, or to separate either of them from Women's Lib. My personal awareness of the problems facing women came in bits and dribbles—once or twice in torrents—sometimes after the fact, and it's only been in the last three or four years, really, that anything has happened to me personally that I saw as a cut-and-dried Lib issue and could relate to the Movement as a whole.

For example, you might argue that the first bit of discrimination in my life came at that time when mom ended my football career and dad told me there were just those three sports—golf, swimming, and tennis—open to me as a woman. Could be. I realize now that my potential athletic career got chopped in half right then, but how many ten-year-old girls thought about sexism, especially in 1954?

Another example. In junior high school the GAA—Girls' Athletic Association—gave you a letter if you played certain sports, like volleyball and things like that. I liked volleyball well enough and the GAA put a lot of pressure on me to play because I was one of the best athletes in school. But by then I was already taking tennis lessons every day of the week and I played the year round. That's really what I wanted to do. So I asked the head of the GAA if my tennis could count toward my GAA letter. No way. Tennis wasn't a GAA sport. That was discrimination, all right, but I felt it was discrimination against tennis, not against me. I see now the GAA was really saying that tennis just wasn't one of those things little girls could do the year round, in school, at least. Little boys could play tennis in junior high, but not little girls, not even in Southern California.

Or later, in high school. Jerry Cromwell (the boy who'd begun lessons with Clyde Walker about the same time I did) and I kept telling the principal of our school about the benefits of tennis—the travel and all that—and how great it would be if more kids were interested. All through high school I offered to give clinics, but I only did give one—two days before I left for Wimbledon for the first time. And that was only because a new physical education teacher from San Francisco, a Mrs. Young, took the trouble to find out who I was.

"Are you the tennis player I've been reading about?" she asked.

"Yes, I suppose so."

"Why don't you help us out?"

"I've tried every year, Mrs. Young, but they don't even know I'm alive."

That was discrimination too, but again, it was against me as a tennis player, not as a little girl.

Later, when I started speaking out against the sham-amateurism, hypocrisy, and nonprofessional attitudes of the USLTA and related organizations, I felt I was fighting for all tennis players, men and women. I felt we were all in the same boat, and if changes were made we'd all benefit. Sure, women were getting a lousy deal in tennis, but so were the men. It really wasn't until the early open-tennis years with the pretty obvious prize-money differences and the cutbacks in women's tournaments that I saw clearly that the women's deal was a whole lot lousier than the men's. That's when I started to look around and see what was happening to other women, especially women in sports.

It didn't take long to discover that my own experiences weren't very different at all. I once received a really sad letter from a mother whose daughter had been ridiculed by their local newspaper because she'd had the audacity to say she wanted to be a professional athlete. I don't even remember this girl's particular sport, but it killed me to read both her mother's letter and the newspaper clip. It was just something else that made me realize a double standard has always existed for women, even in sports, where you might figure there'd be a little more tolerance. I've since read about studies proving that women athletes have to be much more success-oriented than men because there's so much more social pressure for us to overcome, and I know for a fact that's true. For years, women who played sports full time into their late twenties, or, God forbid, their early thirties, were considered tough, overly aggressive, probably had too many male genes, and were for sure failures at love—and unfortunately, that kind of stereotyping still goes on. It works the other way too, of course. Male dancers, actors, musicians and the like have the opposite problem, but I don't think it begins to compare. The barriers are slowly falling, and I'd like to think our pro tennis tour has had something to do with it, but the barriers are still there.

Chris Evert is a perfect example of sexism in tennis. When she blew in on the scene in 1971 she was written about not so much because she was a good tennis player (she was) as because she was young and demure; even two years later the press was often more interested in her romance with Jimmy Connors than in reporting on her development as a player. It's okay for a "girl" to be an athlete (in the proper sports of course), like Chris or Evonne Goolagong or all those teenage swimming sensations who come along every four years, but when she becomes a "woman" she'd sure better be ready to get married and return to a "normal" lifestyle, or else. And what follows is that these women shy away from telling other people, like the press, their true feelings about what they're doing because they don't want to risk the criticism. I understand that. It's a natural reaction.

I like being a career woman and I love being an athlete. I *love* it. But I'm not the only one. More and more women are proud of themselves for having chosen a tennis career, and I wish some of the other players, especially the younger ones who still say to me, "You tell 'em how you feel, Billie, and we'll follow," would come out and tell 'em themselves. I think if they did, if they just came out and shouted, "It makes me happy to be a professional athlete," that maybe it would help to erase the sexist thinking that unfortunately still says it's wrong for a woman to be playing tennis when she could be off raising a family somewhere.

There's simply less and less reason for any woman to tie herself down with marriage and kids if she doesn't want to, and in sports, I think we tennis players might have one of the best deals going anywhere. On a per-tournament basis, our prize money—$50,000—is now equal to the men's World Championship Tennis tour, and through the Women's Tennis Association we've been able to help set minimum prize-money standards for other tournaments throughout the world. Sure, there's more overall money available to the men, but there are more men players too. Even that's changing, however. In 1971 there were just those original sixteen women on the Virginia Slims tour; this year, including qualifiers, there are well over 150. That more women are making tennis their lifelong careers (athletically speaking) is also measured by the interesting fact that the average age of the world's top ten players had jumped from not quite twenty-three in 1962 to just over twenty-seven by 1971—the first year of our tour.

It isn't all gravy, however. Although promoters and advertisers are finally starting to realize that women have a big place in the sports-entertainment field, we haven't even begun to put a foot in the door when it comes to outside endorsements. Until my match with Bobby Riggs I would have said without a doubt that players like Arthur Ashe, Stan Smith, and Rod Laver got more endorsement opportunities than I did, simply because they were men. I really firmly believe this. But if I can sell more cola, or more insurance, or more condominiums than they can, then the businessmen and businesswomen responsible for marketing that stuff ought to want me to do it. And not just me, but every other top woman player, too.

Certainly part of this problem is with the women themselves. We've been conditioned to believe that one of the many things men can do better than we can is sell things, which is nonsense, because I'll guarantee you that people like Rosie Casals and Lesley Hunt could sell just as well as most of the men if they put their minds to it. And when they do, when we all do, then any one of us will be able to walk in the door of any business establishment in the country and have them be as receptive to us as they are to the men now. No question about it.

I know I've talked a lot about money, but let me say again that it's by no means at the top of my list of priorities. Money does two things—it buys freedom for me to spend time on other matters besides keeping body and soul together, and it buys recognition for the tour. When I had those two $100,000 years in 1971 and 1972, I'm positive that a lot of people who didn't know anything about women's tennis—including some sports editors—took a look at those six-figure bankrolls and decided we women must be pretty good athletes after all. Didn't that compare with what some of the best male golfers and football, basketball, and baseball players made? And they'd been on top of the sports pages for years. Getting paid well is always an eye-grabber, and I'm also sure those $100,000 seasons were one of the reasons I was named *Sports Illustrated* magazine's first-ever Sportswoman of the Year in 1972.

Incidentally, the *Sports Illustrated* award has an interesting Women's Lib lesson too. John Wooden, the UCLA basketball coach, was Sportsman of the Year and we shared the cover (another *SI* first; we women have to be brought along slowly). At a press conference for the two of us I was asked whether I felt my selection was a token. My answer was no because I honestly thought I'd deserved it, and I pointed out that my selection was a real breakthrough. Obviously it was, since in its nineteen-year history the magazine had managed to do without having ever named a Sportswoman of the Year. I felt it was a step in the right direction because it meant that maybe the most prestigious sports magazine in the world had finally accepted women as a legitimate part of the sports world. And it meant that it had accepted the women's pro tour also. My selection was a three-way triumph: for me, for women's tennis, and for women everywhere.

Still, I don't feel the media give women athletes anywhere near the coverage they deserve, and that's one of the reasons I've started my own sports magazine for women. I don't mean to pick on *Sports Illustrated,* but in my entire career it's given me exactly one feature story and one cover all to myself. How many times has Arnold Palmer been on the cover? Or Joe Namath? Or Kareem Abdul-Jabbar? A lot more than once, I'll tell you. Part of the problem is being a tennis player, but a bigger problem is being a woman athlete.

The women's magazines have their own hangups, too. I remember one photo session for a leading magazine where the photographer tried to pose me in a slinky dress lying across a couch. As Geraldine says, "What you see is what you get," and slinky I'm not, and certainly not to help a magazine perpetuate a stereotyped view of what women are and what women want to be.

WomenSports, I hope, will not only give women athletes the coverage they deserve, but will cover them as athletes who happen to be women, not as decorations or sideshow attractions in the real world of sports.

I think in the back of their minds my parents always figured that I would quit tennis early—I know that's what they hoped—even after I'd been to places like

Wimbledon and Forest Hills a few times, and that I'd settle down and get married to someone who could take care of me for the rest of my life. For a long time, so did I. Remember that essay I wrote about Wimbledon when I was fourteen? Here's the rest of it, when I thought way ahead and imagined my life at the age of forty-five.

. . . Here I am at home twenty-seven years later sitting at home with my four wonderful children. (At times they're wonderful.) After that summer of '61 I entered Pomona College, in California, spending five years, and graduated with a Masters Degree. I married Ramsey Earnhart, remember that boy I met on the way to the plane that day? Even though I never did achieve my ambition in tennis, I'm so glad I went ahead and received a higher education than high school instead of turning out to be a tennis bum. . . .

Incredible, that's what my expectations were—college, marriage, retirement, kids—just the way my parents wanted. They've really had to adjust a lot to accept what I've become. Years later, when Larry was in law school and I was helping out with my earnings from my "amateur" tennis and later from the National Tennis League, my mother still kept telling me she'd never raised me to be a breadwinner. And even now, they both think I should have started in on those four kids and forgotten about the tennis entirely.

I could have gone either way, really, up until 1966, when I started playing full time, and if I'd married somebody besides Larry King I might well have had a more conventional life. But Larry was cool. It's really strange. When we first met, Larry honestly didn't even know I was a tennis player. He thought I was just another friend of Marcos Carriedo, his bridge-playing buddy who'd introduced us at Los Angeles State. He found out in a hurry though, and in a lot of ways he sensed my needs and desires as a tennis player even more fully than I did. Larry was also quick to see the connection between women's tennis and Women's Lib —that the changes I was trying to bring about in my profession were exactly the same as the changes women in other professions had been fighting for in theirs for years. I'm fortunate to be married to a guy like Larry, because a lot of the demands of my career certainly haven't made his life any easier, and I'm sure he realized almost from the start of our marriage that if he'd wound up with somebody else his life might have been a little calmer too.

Our marriage has had a lot of rough spots and I guess in some ways it's been pretty unconventional. Overall, I think we've made the adjustments pretty well, but sometimes other people—everyone from total strangers to our families and some of our friends— haven't been able to adjust at all. In almost nine years of marriage we've found that people react to lifestyles that are different from theirs even more strongly than they do, say, to unconventional sports personalities. If it had been left up to just Larry and me, I'm sure our marriage would have had an easier time of it.

But we never did conform, and our relationship has always suffered by comparison with other marriages, even within tennis. There are two pretty obvious examples, and the first comes from very early in my career.

Karen Hantze, my first doubles partner back in 1961, had what was considered then to be the ideal athletic career, for a woman. A few months after we'd won our first Wimbledon title, she married Rod Susman, a pretty fair circuit player himself but one who never did play much after college because he was more interested in a business career. The next year Karen won the Wimbledon singles title. The year after that she had a child, and in 1964, at the age of twenty-one, she retired. Perfect. She'd played seriously and well—but not too long. She'd won some major championships—but not too many. And she'd finally settled down to becoming a good mother and a loving wife.

When Larry and I got married, however, I kept right on playing, and a lot of people couldn't understand why; they couldn't accept the fact that Karen and I were different kinds of people, and so were Rod and Larry.

For starters, Rod was a pretty jealous guy. Karen used to say that she worried a lot because Rod was afraid she would be going out with other men during those weeks she was on the road alone. I'd just laugh, because there was just no way. Karen was so loyal to him she didn't even look at other men. Larry, on the other hand, was never jealous, and that was a big difference right there.

Rod always felt he had to make it on his own, too, and he had to know he was the one in the family bringing home the bacon. Larry never got hung up on things like that at all.

There were even bigger differences between Karen and me, and the biggest one of all was that she just didn't have the drive to be Number One. On the way back from England after she'd won her singles title she said, "That's the ultimate for me. I never dreamed I would win Wimbledon; I never thought it would happen."

She knew she didn't have the desire to play tennis the rest of her life, and when she retired I said, "Right on. Whatever makes you happy."

So we went our separate ways. The four of us were just completely different people, and it made for two very different kinds of married lifestyles, but for years and years people just couldn't grasp that.

More recently, Larry and I have been compared (mostly unfavorably) with Margaret Court and her husband, Barry. They were married in late 1967, and four years later she dropped off the circuit for eleven months to have her child, Danny. When she started playing again in mid-1972 the three of them were an inseparable fixture on the circuit. Which was great. Barry was a delightful Australian sportsman from Perth who really enjoyed traveling and taking care of Danny while Margaret played, and since it was pretty obvious they had a good thing going, more power to them. But it just wasn't the way that Larry and I could ever have lived—if for no other reason than that he goes bananas if he has to spend more than forty-eight hours in the same city. This time, the comparisons were really vicious, especially after my abortion became big news. I remember in particular one magazine article in 1972. It was an otherwise nice piece, but it ended with an imaginary description of me somehow looking over at Margaret and her baby, and to me at least the implication was clear: There was Margaret who'd given up tennis for almost a year so she could have a baby, and there I was in a real depression because I'd done something I'd feel guilty about the rest of my life.

It wasn't just the comparison that bothered me in this case either. I felt it was another example of the old double standard. Nobody ever writes about the really intimate life of a male athlete. It's usually off limits, just like it is with male politicians and other male public figures. I didn't think I should be treated any differently just because I was a woman.

I'm really freaked about my privacy. Basically, I feel my private life is nobody's business but my own, and I feel sorry for other celebrities who are hounded even more than I am. They've got my full sympathy. I really don't understand why people are interested in what movie stars, or politicians, or athletes do from the moment they get up until they go to bed—and sometimes even after that. Sure, I'll admit being a celebrity can be fun, like after my match with Bobby Riggs when I was written into a couple of comic strips, "Doonesbury" and "The Wizard of Id." That's great. But the gossip-column, *Ball Four* stuff I can do without. Number one, they're usually wrong.. Number two, even if they're right about something, I change my mind so often that whatever the situation is, it's usually totally different by the time a particular item sees print.

I know a lot of things about a lot of people that I'd just never tell anyone because I don't feel I have the right to pass along little intimacies. I feel very strongly about this. And in my case, I know that people can be really cruel because they have been in the past—not all people, of course, but enough of them. If I told absolutely everything I know, even about myself, I really feel I'd be crucified. There are too many people who are just waiting to get back at me, if you want to know the truth.

At the same time, there are some things I'd like to say about my marriage. Larry and I have gone through a lot together. I certainly don't want to suggest we're the ideal couple or anything like that because I don't believe there is any such thing, but after almost nine years of marriage I really do believe we get along together better now than we ever have. There have been a lot of low spots, and even times when we were both ready to cancel everything, but through it all we were both always able to communicate, and I think that's just about the most basic requirement for any relationship, in or out of marriage.

Larry and I should never have gotten married, at least not when we did. We both thought we were ready —I couldn't wait—and I think we both felt that despite my tennis and his law school, we'd eventually get around to a pretty conventional marriage. Maybe not right away, but eventually. But we were both young —he was twenty and I was twenty-one—and so immature in a lot of ways it was unbelievable. And neither one of us had any idea, really, what was going to happen in tennis the next few years. We both agree now we should have just moved in and lived together for a few years to see how things worked out.

We had to adjust a lot the first couple of years because after that first winter when I stayed home and brought him his sandwiches at the factory, we started to lead pretty separate lives and it got lonely for both of us. I think we started to realize pretty early that marriage isn't a fifty-fifty proposition very often—it's more like 100–0 one moment and 0–100 the next. But that was pretty hard to put into practice. I wanted Larry to travel with me on the circuit, but I was afraid to ask him because that would have taken him away from law school, which was his life. We called each other every night and our phone bill was outrageous— it probably would have been cheaper if he'd joined me.

Larry did come to certain tournaments, but that wasn't much better. I wanted to be with him, but I'd have to jump out of bed first thing in the morning to go practice or play or something, and when I wasn't around there just wasn't anything for him to do. He'd read a lot and play tennis himself whenever he could, but mainly he'd get antsy.

Of course, when I went home to Berkeley I wanted our moments together there, right? And I just expected him to drop everything. But by then he was filling up his time alone with various things and it was hard to ask him to drop his little schedule just because I happened to miss a tournament and toodle on home. Our separate routines got so different that it became more and more difficult for us to get back onto the same cycle those few times we were together. We reached the point where we never felt like we were married, like we belonged to each other. I remember he told me once, "Y'know? I'm getting sick and tired of sharing you with the world." And that was a pretty accurate remark about what was going on.

In those first couple of years, we had pretty traditional expectations for each other, and a couple of times I thought seriously of not playing at all any more and just going back to that apartment in Berkeley to be there full time, for him.

The one really good thing that happened during this period was that Larry saw for himself what a mess tennis was in—like when promoters offered to pay his expenses if I would play in their tournaments. That kind of thing was a little awkward for both of us. I didn't want him to feel any smaller because I was getting extra money through him, and he didn't. I was the one who got off on that stuff. He felt a little strange, sure, but mainly he saw there was a tremendous opportunity in tennis for anyone with even a little bit of business sense. And in 1968 he started in as a promoter. He took our life savings, all $5,000 of it, and with a bunch of other law students from Cal put on a tournament in the Oakland Coliseum Arena. Made a little bit too, and he's been in tennis full time almost ever since.

I think our worst moment together was in 1969, right after he graduated from law school. It seems like a pretty small thing now, but it really shows where we were then. He wanted to live in Hawaii. I said fine, but right away I was miserable, for a lot of reasons. That made my plane trip to the East Coast eleven hours, and that's a killer. And the East was also where most of the tournaments were. In the Islands they couldn't care less about pro sports—all they're interested in is high school football—and there I was working my you-know-what off as a professional athlete. There just wasn't anything there for me. So I'd bop into town for a week and it was great when he had time off, but he was just starting to practice law then and didn't have much time off. When he did, he liked to go swimming. I didn't, but I'd go lie on the beach and get a suntan. Fair enough. You can't like everything. At night we'd occasionally go out with other lawyers and their wives. Another problem. I just couldn't handle the social chatter again.

I felt lost whenever I was there, and I felt that Larry and I were on different levels completely. I could maybe take being away from him, but when we were together we had to have something in common. Enough was enough.

We eventually moved back to Berkeley—two years later—but I think that summer in Hawaii was the first time I started thinking about divorce. Over the next four years I thought about it a lot, and by the end of 1973, I was ready—we both were. You've got to remember that by then I'd been through an awful lot of things with my career—open tennis and the National Tennis League tour, the Virginia Slims circuit, a couple of pretty good playing years, and the Riggs match. It was go-go-go all the time and I wanted a change. We didn't get a divorce then, and now I don't think we will, but the things that were going through my mind then were pretty revealing.

If we had separated, it wouldn't have been a traditional divorce at all, because I'm pretty sure we would have kept on living together. Considering the amount of traveling we both did and the time we were already apart, even a divorce wouldn't have changed our geographic relationship very much at all.

I still loved Larry and I knew I always would. And I knew Larry loved me. Larry and I always disagreed on one important thing, however, which was maybe only a matter of semantics. He said "love" was liking someone the most; I thought "love" was "love" and "like" was "like" and that they were both very different. I understood what he was saying—I think the difference was that he's simply not as emotional as I am—but I didn't agree with him. Maybe I was old-fashioned, but to me, love was really indescribable; it was that feeling of something extra, something special.

However we defined it, though, we both knew that love was something that changed constantly. It was never the same from one day to the next. I was happier than I'd ever been in my life, even with all the crazy things that had been going on around me, but I felt that now we had a different kind of relationship from the one we'd started out in, and that maybe it required a different kind of love. What I felt was almost just the opposite of hate, or of wanting to scratch his eyes out. It was the sense that we were two mature people, which we hadn't been eight years before, and that because of the way we lived we both needed a sense of personal freedom that we'd never really had before. A lot happens to you in your twenties. Even though we'd been apart geographically, we were always very close emotionally, maybe so close that I just hadn't been able to absorb and sort out all the changes that had happened to me. I wouldn't have minded being alone for awhile —and then starting over with Larry. I felt it would have been like meeting a stranger—but someone I knew I'd love and admire right from the first.

I also felt it would have made things much easier for me because of people on the outside who didn't understand our relationship at all. People drove me nuts. They were asking the same questions they'd asked for eight years: Where is your husband? Doesn't he travel with you? When are you going to retire? Don't you want kids? And on and on. I didn't like that. It's like they were chipping away at me, always expecting me to live up to their own expectations rather than mine. If I were single again, I felt, a lot of those questions would stop, or at least my answers would make more sense to others.

Did I want kids? Sure, by the time I was thirty-five, just for my own healthy, bodily reasons. But it didn't make any difference any more if I had them in or out of marriage. I knew that would blow everybody's mind. How could I want a divorce and *then* want kids?

My parents were just completely in love with children, and to them the family unit was the beginning and the end. Here Randy and I had just excelled at what we'd done and I knew they felt one of the reasons was that they'd given us the time and the love and the attention, and they were absolutely right. They'd done a great job. But times had changed, and I couldn't raise my kids in the same fashion. Yet, when the time came for me I was sure I'd have the guilts if I didn't raise my own kids the same way I was brought up. It's hard to change your conditioning no matter how right on you think your thinking is.

But right then, I didn't feel marriage was where it was at—at least not in the traditional sense.

Well, we didn't get a divorce and I'm not sure why, except we just stopped talking about it. There was one very practical reason though. During the winter of 1973–74 I was caught up in the aftermath of my match with Riggs, I was trying to get my magazine, *women-Sports,* off the ground, and I was also working into shape for the 1974 Virginia Slims tour. For his part, Larry was tied up with World Team Tennis almost daily. Even if we had finally decided to go ahead with it, I think neither one of us would have had the time to file the papers.

More important, I think we've since come to a pretty solid understanding about where our relationship is. He's got his career and I've got mine, and they're like two big intersecting circles. At those points where they meet, everything's great. Where they don't meet—what can I say? Except we can both handle it because we know that's just the way things are going to be for a few more years.

* * *

I got pregnant in late February, 1971—dollars to donuts, the night before the finals of the Women's National Indoors in Winchester, Massachusetts. I am sure, I am *positive* it was then because the next day I started getting hot flashes on the court. I thought—I hoped—I was getting sick. No such luck. In the next few days coffee started smelling bad and tasting worse, and when we got to New York three weeks later, I knew. I just knew.

I lost to Rosie Casals in the finals and I felt terrible. I thought I was going to vomit the entire match. I couldn't run at all. Rosie would hit a drop shot and all I could do was wave my hand feebly and say, "Nice shot."

By then, Larry was back in California. I called him, told him the news, and flew home.

I took the usual tests, and when they came out positive, there was absolutely no question about what I would do. We agreed on an abortion from the beginning, and there was very little thinking about the morality involved in our decision. If that sounds shocking, all I can do is plead honesty. I mean I did believe strongly that inexpensive, legal abortions ought to be available to every woman, and since I was only about a month pregnant I didn't feel I was killing a life or anything like that. But the real reason for my decision was that I also felt it was absolutely the wrong time for me to bring a child into the world. Even though Larry and I had been married for five and a half years, we'd been living a strange, disjointed life and I felt we needed more time together by ourselves to see where our relationship was headed. I was entering a period of great change in my life, personally and professionally, and under the circumstances I felt it just wasn't proper to start a family. Finally, I didn't want to become a mother unless I could devote myself fully to the job, and I knew that was something I just couldn't do, not yet. So I decided to go ahead with the abortion. It's a decision I've never regretted.

In California it usually takes ten days to arrange for an abortion, but the doctor was a friend of a friend and got things together in four or five. Larry, as my husband, had to sign the permission papers, which we both felt was wrong, and it cost $580, which was absolutely ridiculous. I could certainly afford it, but that's a lot of money for most women who want and need abortions. My operation was so simple that it could easily have been performed by a competent nurse and probably shouldn't have cost more than $25 or $30. It was the simplest operation I've ever had. I went to the hospital, was knocked out, had the abortion, spent two hours in a recovery room, and then Larry took me home. Done. It didn't begin to compare with either of my knee operations, and later that year when I had some wisdom teeth yanked, the pain and the agony were much worse. There was no trauma at all. I just wanted to get it over with.

The immediate reaction was pretty quiet. I only told about two or three people, and although that was enough to get the word around to the other women on the tour, nobody ever said much. It was sort of a taboo subject, I guess, and I wasn't about to volunteer too much information myself. So things stayed calm. What happened a year later, though, was something else.

The legalization of abortion was now a big issue all over the country and to help dramatize it *Ms.* magazine ran a petition under a headline that said, WE HAVE HAD ABORTIONS. It was signed by fifty-three women, and I was one of them. This petition had come in the mail a few weeks earlier and Larry gave it to me. "You'll probaby want to sign this," he said, "it's about legalized abortion." Good stuff. Fine. So I signed. I was almost sure the petition said that we signees were only in favor of legalized abortion, *not* that we'd had abortions ourselves. (It turned out that *Ms.* didn't know for sure itself that all the women who signed the petition had, in fact, had an abortion. It was relying on the politics of the women it solicited.)

On February 8, 1972, Bud Collins quietly put two and two together in the Boston *Globe* and wrote, ". . . [Billie Jean King] was so busy winning and earning and trying to make the women's pro tour succeed that she decided not to take time out to start a family. Billie Jean's abortion was made public in a declaration. . . ."

In the next couple of weeks I started getting some feedback from people who'd seen either Bud's column or the petition itself. But nothing I couldn't handle.

Then, two weeks later, the tour hit Washington, D.C., and as I said before, that was just about the worst week in my life. Mark Asher, the tennis writer for the Washington *Post,* asked me flat out in an interview before the tournament began whether I'd had an abortion. I told him I was there to promote a tennis tournament and to play in it, and I didn't think his question was relevant to that.

He said he was sorry, but that he had to ask. I said I believed that women ought to have control over their own bodies, that I was strongly in favor of legalized abortions, and that's why I signed the petition. I said as to whether I'd actually had an abortion, he'd have to come to his own conclusions.

Finally, I asked him to please not write about the abortion issue at all, as a personal favor to me.

I didn't lie to Asher, but I'll admit I did hedge on my answer. For three reasons. First, although I was certainly in favor of legalized abortion, I really didn't think it was anybody's business whether I'd had one myself unless I chose to announce it personally. Second, it was now almost a full year since my operation and I felt it was old news. Finally, I'd told very few people about it, and among those I hadn't told were my parents, because I was sure they just wouldn't understand.

Well, the next day the *Post* ran Mark's story eight columns wide across the top of its sports section under the headline: "Abortion Made Possible Mrs. King's Top Year." In fairness to Mark, his story never quoted me as saying I'd had an abortion, but the damage was done.

I lost to Julie Heldman in a sloppy match in the round of sixteen. Afterward, there was the usual press conference, and when Asher walked in I saw red. That's all there was to it. I felt he'd betrayed me and broken a trust, and I couldn't even believe he'd had the guts to show up. That was the final blow to a lousy winter and a devastating week. I think I felt every negative emotion in the book. But it was really strange. It was as though there was this part of me outside my body like Big Brother or Big Sister or something, watching me go through all of this rage, depression, anger—you name it.

I refused to talk to the press until Asher left. He wouldn't, and I walked out. I'd had it, and almost immediately, Larry and I flew to Hawaii. When we got off the plane, the first headline I saw was: "Tennis Star Has Abortion."

Asher's story had been sent out on the Washington *Post*–Los Angeles *Times* wire and was getting big play everywhere. I couldn't have felt worse, because I knew what must be happening back in Long Beach.

So there it was, my parents first found out in the newspaper, not from me.

Several weeks later I went home for Mother's Day. I still hadn't talked to either mom or dad about it. Chicken. I just couldn't bring myself to do it. Mom and I sat down to watch television because there was a long segment about me on "60 Minutes" that we wanted to see. That came and went uneventfully and was followed by another long segment—on abortions.

That broke the dam and I could have died. Mom said she'd cried for three days when she first heard about it. She asked me if I loved kids. She asked me if I loved Larry. She said she trusted me but she just couldn't understand.

I told her I didn't expect her to understand, that Larry and I had our reasons—personal reasons I didn't want to go into—and through it all I was mainly sorry I hadn't had the guts to tell her first myself.

The hate mail was coming in by then too, letters from people who called me a killer and, predictably I guess, refused to sign their names. In all, it was a pretty grim period.

But overall, I've seen a lot of good come from it. Several women have told me that just knowing I'd had an abortion and was willing to speak out about it—however reluctantly at first—made it easier for them to have theirs, and that's a really big plus. I don't expect everybody to accept what I did, but that's all right because I don't ever want to go around putting my own standards about anything on other people. I can't help thinking, though, that if somebody in my position had spoken out five years earlier about abortion, it might have made it a whole lot easier for me to deal with mine when the time came.

What is my position? I'm not really sure. I'm not going to be too humble about this—why start now?—but I'm honestly amazed sometimes by the way people react to me. I mean like especially after the excitement of that perfect night in Houston when I beat Bobby Riggs and just plain went over the top, I think, as a public figure. You wouldn't believe the number of people who have got to tell me exactly what they did, wherever they were, as they watched the match.

Like the women at Mount Holyoke College who clustered around a dormitory television set shouting, "Right on!" after practically every point.

Or the magazine editor, a woman, who was supposed to have dinner ready on the table but wound up at a party at *Ms.* magazine—where Bella Abzug waved her floppy hat almost the whole night—and finally called her husband: "Dear . . . darling . . . Billie Jean's ahead. I won't be home until after the match."

Or, the group at a country club bar in South Carolina, mostly men, who actually stood up and applauded the TV set, the *TV set,* when I was finished with Bobby.

Sure, the match grabbed everybody, but people had been reacting to me very strongly long before that. It began, really, about the end of 1971, after the Virginia Slims circuit had been under way for almost a year. Women especially really started to look up to me then, I think because they realized how much the tour and I had fought to get where we were.

Dick Butera, the president of the Philadelphia Freedoms of World Team Tennis, keeps telling me I have an effect on people without even thinking about it, and I guess he's right. I know I'm in a close to unique position and combined with my constitutional let's-change-the-world attitude, it makes for pretty powerful medicine, but boy, sometimes it really makes me nervous.

Sometimes I'm totally amazed by the things that happen. About two weeks after I played Riggs, I went to the Philadelphia *Bulletin* for a press conference. I must have met everybody in the building, and I talked to most of them—just small talk, nothing serious. I found out later, though, that the morning after the match with Bobby several of the women there had stormed into their bosses' offices, and demanded raises on the spot. I couldn't believe it, but I thought it was great.

It's a funny feeling to know that women look up to me, but that's one of the ways Women's Lib has changed things. Women aren't ashamed of identifying with other women. It's always been all right for a guy to look up to another guy, but it's hardly ever been okay for a woman to look up to another woman, because we were taught that men were the only successful and wonderful people in the world. The big reason was probably a lack of examples, but I think we're getting a bunch of our own now.

It's a two-way street. Maybe women look up to me, and that's fine, but in the last couple of years especially I've really tried to talk with other women too. I've tried to find out about their lives and their problems, and I think I've learned a lot.

The two basic things I've learned are these: We women are all the same, in the sense that somewhere along the line we've just about all of us encountered some kind of sexist discrimination either in our careers or in our personal lives, and probably in both. Some of us have been lucky and have had either the opportunity or some kind of inner strength to fight back and make a little niche for ourselves. Most of us haven't been so fortunate, however, and that's why mutual support among women is so important. Because although things are changing, they're changing slowly, and it's a pretty good bet we're not going to get too much help from anybody except ourselves.

The other thing I've learned is that we women are all different in our desires and our expectations. One of us might want a career, another a family life, and still a third might want both. We might want to swing or we might not want to swing at all. The important thing is for us to be able to do our thing with respect and dignity, to be able to lead the fullest possible lives we can, and to find the center of ourselves.

Liberalized abortion laws? Yes. An end to job discrimination? Of course. Equal pay for equal work? No question. But those are details. What really counts is for us to be able to fulfill our potential in whatever way we choose. And the awareness of that possibility, that right, is only the beginning; the achievement is the end.

9

I've Come a Long Way,
Bobby: The Riggs Match

ON MAY 13, 1973—Mother's Day—Rosie Casals, Marilyn Barnett, my personal secretary, and I were on a flight from Tokyo to Los Angeles, returning from a tournament in Japan. All of us were keyed up. There was a match being played that Sunday afternoon near San Diego, California, and we were desperate to find out the score. We landed in Honolulu, a short layover, and literally ran into the airport terminal. They've got all those little television sets, right? So I put my little quarters in. Nothing. No tennis. Reruns of "Gunsmoke" or something. Turns out they delay everything in Hawaii a week. We just flipped. Rosie was running around, I was going crazy, kicking the TVs, and Marilyn was trying to calm us both down. Finally Marilyn remembered Rosie's super tape recorder–radio and turned it on. We just got the last part of a sports report: "Bobby Riggs beat Margaret Court today, 6–2, 6–1." What can I say? I went bananas. None of us could believe it. No way. Right then and there I said, "That's it. I've got to play him." The moment I heard those scores, *6–2, 6–1*, I knew I *had* to play Bobby Riggs. The door had been

*I couldn't believe how slow Riggs was.
I thought he was faking it. He had to
be. At the change after the first game
I asked Dennis, "He's putting me on,
right?" Dennis assured me I was seeing
the real thing.*

----

opened and things were out of my control. It was only
a matter of time and place and money.

Until 1971 I'd never met Bobby Riggs or even seen
him play, but everybody in tennis knew his record and
reputation. Bobby never had a power game, but he was
one of the best ball-control artists of all time and won
Wimbledon once, in 1939, and Forest Hills twice, 1939
and 1941. He lost a lot of good years to World War II,
turned professional, and like all professionals in those
days, dropped out of sight. Riggs was a hustler from the
beginning. Clyde Walker, my first coach, told me many
stories about this little punk who used to come out to
the courts around Los Angeles and hustle matches when
he was thirteen. He was a compulsive gambler. In 1939
he bet £100 on himself to win the Wimbledon singles
(betting's legal in England) and when he won that he
let the money ride through the doubles and the mixed.
He got the slam—and over $100,000. At country clubs
he'd play handicap matches—give some local guy a few
points a game or a few games a set—and usually win.
And when he got tired of that he started in with the

gimmicks. He'd play while walking a dog on a leash, or in an overcoat, or with chairs placed on his side of the court: "How many chairs you want?"

So when he came out with his first challenge, in 1971, I had a pretty good idea what he was up to. He wanted to play for $5,000 or something like that, winner take all, and he was already into his Male Chauvinist Pig thing. He claimed *any* man could beat *any* woman, that the women's game was dull compared to the men's, and that there was no reason for us to get equal prize money. I don't know how serious he was about all of that back then or even how serious he is now, but the hustler in him must have sensed the possibilities in a "Battle of the Sexes" match right from the beginning. At Forest Hills that year I remember I was practicing on the Clubhouse court one day when he suddenly came out of nowhere, jumped over the little fence by the court, and kept saying to me, "You've got to play. How can you not want to play?"

I turned him down, cold. At that time my mind was only concerned with getting the Virginia Slims circuit on the road, nothing else. We were trying to prove that women could make it on their own and I didn't want to get anything started that might distract from that goal. I didn't think that any of us women needed to play against an older man, and even if we did, just what was it gonna prove? If we played and I won, so what? I beat somebody twenty-five years older than me. If I lost, Bobby would carry that MCP thing on forever—or at least until somebody did beat him.

The odds were lousy. Our circuit was struggling then, and if Bobby had won, just enough people might have believed his spiel to send our whole tour down the drain. It was that touchy.

He kept saying what a great hype our match would be for the women's tour, but I told him that if we couldn't make it on our own then we didn't deserve to make it at all. I more or less told him we didn't want him.

And so the whole thing died until February, 1973, when he issued another challenge through the newspapers. It was the same old stuff. "The women couldn't take more than one or two games a set from the good men's players . . . So why should they be paid the same as men? . . . The women are getting more money than they deserve, anyway. . . ." Etc., etc., etc.

I still didn't want to play him. Our tour was coming along pretty well by then, but still, what would it prove? So I turned him down again, even though Larry felt there was a good chance I could make somewhere between $35,000 and $50,000 from the match. But then the public got interested—got very demanding, in fact—and Jackie Barnett, Bobby's agent, got in touch with Larry. Before anything serious could happen, though, the first week in March, Margaret Court announced to a group of us in the dressing room at Cobo Hall in Detroit that *she* was going to play—for a $5,000 guarantee and another $5,000 if she won.

Margaret was really excited. She felt that was a lot of money for just one day of tennis and I didn't say too much to discourage her because she was so happy. But I tried to warn her. "It's not just a one-day deal, Margaret," I said. "It's gonna be a six-week deal." I didn't think she understood how hectic things would get for her.

I was disappointed she was going to play him at all, and even more disappointed that the money was so little. She was literally putting her name and the reputation of women's tennis on the line—at least that's how I knew the public would look at it no matter how she or the rest of us felt personally—and all for a dinky $5,000, maybe $10,000. (She did eventually get the $10,000, even though she lost.)

I really wanted Margaret to win, for herself and for

us, and I thought that she at least had a good chance. There were a handful of women who could have beaten him and she was definitely among them. But whatever happened, I wanted the match to be good, and entertaining. Unfortunately, it wasn't.

Although I didn't see the match myself, I caught a tape of it a week or so later at a television studio in Savannah and I almost got sick. Did she do a nerve job? Oh, yeah, without a doubt. The psych began when Riggs handed her those flowers before the match and never let up. I could tell after she hit two balls what was happening. It just killed me to see it. It kills me to see any athlete have that bad a day. I mean, you want to see both players play great and just whoever has the better day win. That kind of crackup happens to everybody one or two times in his or her career and it's just unfortunate that it hit her on that particular day. I felt sorry for her and I think there must have been great sympathy for her from everybody who watched the match. But it really made me sick, and it made me stop and think what I was getting myself into, which was good.

I think Margaret was genuinely surprised at how much interest the match caused, like I told her in Detroit. Funny, she just didn't understand what was happening. When we women play each other in tournaments we just go out and play; we don't give out with all that razzmatazz like Bobby did. Then, too, Margaret's at her best when she's playing for herself without any outside pressures. The thing got so big that by the time the match started I don't think she knew what was going on.

What went wrong technically is that first of all Margaret didn't go to the net enough. But to play the big game your timing's got to be perfect, and when you get as nervous as Margaret got, your timing is the first thing to go. So Margaret had to stay back, and that's not her best game. Also, when she stayed back she played in too close to the base line. Bobby hits pretty deep and on every shot Margaret would have to run back a little way to hit the return. Then she'd move in again, then have to move back again. That gets pretty tiring after awhile. Finally, Margaret has "bad hands." She doesn't have a whole lot of touch. Most of the time she gets away with it because she can just overwhelm everybody with her power and her great reach. But if she's got to play another kind of style she's in trouble, especially if it involves finesse. So those are the three things that beat her—nerves, not being able to play her game, and no touch.

I only talked with Margaret about the match once. That was in Nashville five weeks before I played Riggs. Even then I felt funny asking her about it. I knew it would be a sore point with her and I really didn't know whether she wanted me to win or not. She said she didn't remember a whole lot about the match, which I could understand, but one thing she did tell me was that Riggs couldn't hit through his backhand very well. That is, he couldn't hit over the ball with much power from that side and so had to rely on placement almost entirely.

That was useful information, because before he and I played I really knew very little about him. I'd never played him, of course, so there was no track record to go on, and his match with Margaret was so one-sided that even seeing the tapes didn't tell me much. It was obvious he hadn't played anywhere near his best, wherever that is.

Riggs's people got in touch with my people again almost immediately after the Court match and in late June, just before Wimbledon, we signed to play. We announced the match on July 11, and from that moment on, right up until the time we stepped on the court in the middle of the Houston Astrodome on the night of September 20, life was one big circus. The contract was unsettled from the beginning and in fact the final details weren't fixed until the very day before the match. I'll talk about that a little later, but the basic terms were these: $100,000 in prize money to the winner, plus about another $100,000 in guarantees and ancillary rights to be split evenly between us. Everything else that came along, before the match, was to be split fifty-fifty too. The endorsement offers started to pour in almost immediately, but Bobby and I said no to all of them except Sunbeam (for a hair drier television commercial) and Sugar Daddy. And basically that was it.

From the very first I wanted the match to be the best of five sets, and Bobby agreed. Most people thought a long match would work to my advantage (the Court match had been best of three), but at the time I have to admit I really didn't think it would. I'd been sick and injured a lot that year, and the longer the match, the better the odds were of something else happening to me. But I also didn't want there to be any loopholes for him if I won, none of this, "Well, it was only a three-set match and I could have taken her in five." One of the things Riggs kept egging me on about was how we women couldn't stand up physically to men in a long match, and I felt that if we played best-of-five it would be more convincing.

The hoopla began immediately and didn't let up for ten weeks. And I'd warned Margaret the whole thing would take six! What the media didn't generate, Riggs supplied himself with all that nonsense talk about his vitamin pill popping, his special diets, and with his entourage of honeys to keep up the MCP image. He made scores of public appearances, and the match was written about in almost every newspaper and magazine in the country, maybe the world. We both knew it was a one-shot deal, especially if I won, but, otherwise, each of us treated the match very differently. I was deadly serious about it; for him it was the ultimate ego trip, a vehicle for a super hustler to carry off (he hoped) the ultimate hustle. He knew it was a hustle, I knew it was a hustle, the media knew it was a hustle, and, no mistake, so did the 30,472 people who saw the match live in the Astrodome and the 40 million who saw it on television. In a way that's part of what made the thing so perfect, the thought that everybody else was having a ball and the idea that what we were doing was great for tennis, just great. Sure, it was a one-shot deal, but on that night, I think, the game of tennis finally got kicked out of the country clubs forever and into the world of real sports, where everybody could see it.

But still I tried to stay somewhat away from the show biz atmosphere that was building up. Two reasons. First, compared to other athletes, Bobby's pretty easy to figure out, to get into his mind and understand how he thinks, and I realized the one thing Bobby wanted me to do was get caught up in everything. He's a hustler, but in order to hustle you he's got to see you, know where you are, keep tabs on you. I felt if I hid from him, if I wasn't around physically, it would drive him nuts. And so I stayed out of sight, especially in the last two or three weeks. Second, I knew in the match itself I was going to expend more nervous energy than I ever had before, and using up nervous energy is a lot harder on you than just wearing yourself out physically. So I gave very few interviews and no autographs and tried to keep to myself and stick to my regular routine.

I wanted to be able to analyze the match strictly from an athlete's point of view. I felt if I got caught up in public opinion and all the whoopteedoo it would slant my feelings toward the match instead of letting me look at it as simply as I could—as a contest between him and me and that's all. I felt if I started to listen to every Tom, Dick, and Harry that came along I'd be so confused by the time I walked into the Astrodome I wouldn't have any idea what I was there for. In some respects the match was going to be the most important one in my career, and I wanted to keep that in mind right up to the last moment.

I'm jumping a little bit ahead of myself because these are the things I felt most intensely in the two weeks just before our match. Before that, however, came the U.S. Open at Forest Hills, a tournament I've never really liked. What happened there didn't do much to change my opinion.

Funny, it was actually one of the few times in my career I felt really good about Forest Hills when the tournament started. The women's prize money was equal to the men's at a major event for the first time in the history of open tennis, thanks to a special equalizer purse put up by Ban deodorant, and I was playing so well that I felt I had a good chance to make up for what had been a pretty erratic year. There was a late-summer heat wave that lasted the entire first week of the tournament and most of the second, and I love playing in hot weather. I beat Peggy Michel easily in the first round and I beat Karen Krantzcke on the Stadium court in the second round and lost just four games.

Then that night, after the Krantzcke match, the bottom started to fall out. I got a sore throat and a fever. I was okay as long as I was lying down, but whenever I stood up I had that flu feeling, when everything hurts. I felt awful, in fact. I kept ignoring it, hoping it would go away. But it didn't. Then the heat got worse and so did I. By the time the third round started, though, I still felt if I could just get through one more match I'd be okay. Then I'd have a day off before the quarter finals, and besides, at that point I couldn't feel any worse. I had to get better, right?

In the third round, the round of sixteen, I played

Julie Heldman on the Clubhouse court, the one right in front of the West Side Tennis Club's veranda. Later, everybody said I was unhappy with the court assignment, that I felt the match should have been played in the Stadium or the Grandstand, but I really didn't think too much about it—except I knew a lot of people would be inconvenienced. The spectators were already packed pretty deep by the time Julie and I walked out to play.

I won the first set, 6–3, but I was struggling. I guess no one could tell by watching, but I knew I was. The energy output was tremendous, and in the second set I started to feel—oh, God—everything. The ball felt like five tons, my racket felt like six, and the sky started to spin. I got chills and started thinking I'd never ever felt this lousy before.

I actually got a 4–1 lead in the second set but I don't know how, and I don't remember much of anything after that except thinking, "Hold on. Just hold on. If you get through this match everything'll be all right." Julie sensed I wasn't feeling too hot, that I couldn't run anymore—I must have looked like I was playing in slow motion—and began playing more forcefully. That was the end. She won five games in a row to run out the second set and quickly built a 4–1 lead in the third. I tried, but I couldn't see and I thought I was going to pass out. By then the match was over, and I suppose all I wanted to do was stay on the court until the end, for Julie's benefit because it seems to me no player feels a real victory if she wins by default. All I remember is wanting to just go through the motions and not default and hope I didn't faint in the middle of the court. That would have been real cute.

I guess I began to take more than the one-minute rest period you're allowed on the change of sides. I felt it was better to take some extra time and try to stay on the court until the end, but Julie was getting really ticked off with me, I guess, from what everybody says. I don't remember; everything was very foggy. At 4–1 in the third, when we were both near the umpire's chair, I do remember that Julie said to the umpire, "Sixty seconds. She's gotta play."

The umpire asked me if I was all right. I said something like, "To be honest, no."

Julie said, "C'mon, what are you doing? Play. Play or get off the court." That kind of talk. I remember that.

I told her I really wasn't feeling very well, but what I was really trying to tell her was, "Look, dummy, I'm trying to finish this match for you. There's no way I can win it because I can hardly stand up as it is. Give me my time and we'll get through whatever games are left."

But Julie was really adamant and I didn't know what to do. The umpire didn't say anything, Julie kept shouting, and finally I said, "Julie, if you want it that bad, dammit, you can have it." And I defaulted. I didn't want to, but I felt she put me in a position where I didn't have any choice, and I don't know why she did that. She's a weird, mixed-up person sometimes.

It turned out my immediate problem was that I was getting a bad reaction to the penicillin I was taking for my virus. A doctor said later that if I'd continued, even for those last couple of games, there's a good chance I would have collapsed.

The default was bad for me, but worse for my match with Riggs, which was now just three weeks off. And, God, what rumors! That I'd thrown the match, for example, to have more time to prepare for Bobby, or that if I was sick at all the whole thing was psychosomatic and probably brought on by Bobby's magic powers somehow. Well, all I can say is that I didn't throw the match and, psychosomatic or not, I was sick as a dog and there's no way I could have gone on.

There were also stories that I was using my sickness

as an excuse to get out of the match entirely, and I understand I even lost a *Newsweek* cover because its editors felt the thing might not come off. Again, not true. As a matter of fact, I kept playing the rest of the tournament, and Rosie Casals and I reached the women's doubles finals and Owen Davidson and I won the mixed.

I still wasn't feeling too hot, though. Forest Hills ended on Sunday, September 9. I flew to Hilton Head, South Carolina, that night and the next morning at 10 o'clock played Chris Evert in the first round of a tournament ABC was televising to be shown the following spring. And the same thing happened. I got up a set and 5–2 in the second and almost collapsed all over again. I had her two match points and double-faulted on both of them. I was shaking, not from nerves, but from whatever it was I had picked up at Forest Hills, and I lost to her in three sets.

That was the end, though. I finally got over my virus and by the next Sunday, four days before the match, I was totally okay. No excuses.

At Hilton Head, a posh resort on the Carolina seacoast, the atmosphere was really great. It's a nice place to begin with, and I was able to isolate myself relatively easily from the press and anyone else I didn't want to see. The only people around were Larry, who flew in and out, Annalee Thurston, a secretary at King Enterprises, and Dick Butera, president of the Philadelphia Freedoms, who had become a very close friend in the short time I'd known him. That was all. We went out to dinner together, and to the movies, and listened a lot to the radio.

But mainly, when I wasn't playing tennis, we just sat around and talked about the match while Annalee answered the phone and told people I was busy. I was hyper the whole time, very intense. I lived in a condominium apartment by the golf course, and in the morning the first thing I'd do was get up and walk outside by myself, maybe hit a few golf balls, and try to think through exactly what the whole thing meant, to me, personally. And then I'd talk with Dick and Larry and Annalee some more. By then the television promo spots on ABC were coming hot and heavy and it was really sinking in how much of a happening the whole match was turning into. I remember watching the college game of the week (Stanford versus Penn State) the Saturday before the match when at half time the Stanford University band formed the letters "B J K" and played "I Am a Woman." I honest-to-God got teary-eyed.

Okay, the match was a spectacle, but in a sense it was also the culmination of the second phase of my career. The first had been the fight to become the Number One player in the world. I'd done that. The second was the fight for equality for the women's tour, and in the space of just a few weeks it seemed like that fight was being won. First, the Virginia Slims and USLTA women's pro circuits had just merged and we knew our tournaments would pay $50,000 each the next winter—same as the WCT men's tour. Second, Forest Hills had offered that equal prize money. Third, the television tournament at Hilton Head had paid $40,000 to the winner—Margaret Court—the largest top prize ever in women's tennis. And fourth—the Riggs match. He and a lot of other men are still talking about how much he did for women's tennis by playing Margaret and then me. But —and this is an important point—there's no way our match could have had the impact it did if I hadn't made a name for myself first, and the place I'd done that was on the women's tour—our tour. If we had played even three years before we did, our match wouldn't have made half the splash it did. It was only because women's tennis had come along so far. We gave old Bobby a vehicle with which to exploit himself; it was almost like a marriage situation. And I think that's being as fair as I can about the whole thing.

So it was important to me that the match be straight up and on the level, and that everything about it be exactly right. And because I felt that way it almost fell through—twice.

The original contract was with Jackie Barnett, the guy who'd handled the Riggs–Court match. Then Jerry Perenchio, another Los Angeles promoter who had helped put together the first Muhammad Ali–Joe Frazier fight, got interested and bought out Barnett.

So far so good, except one day in Hilton Head Marilyn Barnett called to say she'd heard from some of her Los Angeles friends that Riggs was getting a piece of the gate. I blew up. I was edgy anyway, maybe even subconsciously looking for a way out, and that was in clear violation of our agreement. I said, "That's it. The match is off. Bad vibes. Call Perenchio. I want to tell him."

Dick Butera said, "Billie, you can't cancel on a rumor. Let me talk to Jerry."

Perenchio was in Los Angeles and caught the next plane East. By the time he arrived I had about nine different reasons why we shouldn't play the match and I lit into him as soon as he got in the car at the airport and didn't let up until we'd finished dinner at a little restaurant in Sea Pines. Perenchio was cool. He told me the thing about Riggs and the gate just wasn't true and he had the right answers to all the other questions I asked him. That took care of that.

But the problems weren't really over yet. ABC had hired three announcers to do the match, Howard Cosell for play-by-play, Rosie Casals for women's color, and Jack Kramer for men's color. I'd told Roone Arledge, the head of ABC Sports, from the beginning that I would not play the match if Kramer was in the broadcasting booth that night. Kramer and I had been going at each other for years and not just because of my walk-out at the Pacific Southwest tournament two years before. Kramer, I felt, just didn't like women's tennis, never had and never would, and I wasn't about to give him a national forum to spout off his views on the night of maybe the biggest match in my life.

Arledge knew how I felt three weeks before we ever got to Houston, but when we did, Kramer was still ABC's guy.

Tuesday night about 1 A.M.—two days before the match—Roone called me. I was asleep and Larry intercepted the call.

Roone said he couldn't fire Kramer. Larry went through my arguments again.

"Get Billie Jean up," Roone said. "I want to talk to her."

"I won't do it," said Larry, "but I warn you, she's not kidding around."

The next afternoon—Wednesday—a meeting was scheduled to firm up the special ground rules for our match. I said I wasn't going to go to it unless I knew Kramer was off the air, because if he wasn't, there was no point talking about rules and I didn't want to waste my time.

We agreed to meet in one of the Astrodome offices—Roone and his people, and me and mine.

I said, "Hi."
He said, "Hi."
I said, "Roone, you've known for at least three weeks how I feel about Kramer and I really would appreciate it if you would get him off. I don't want him there. No way."

"What do you mean, 'No way?' " Roone asked.
"I mean no way. I'm not gonna play."
"C'mon," he said. "You're gonna play."
"Roone, if he's in that TV booth when I walk out on

216

the court I'm not gonna play. I've waited too long not to have things right now. This is my night and Bobby's night, not Jack Kramer's night."

All the time Roone was looking at me like, "God, this kid's crazy, letting a chance like this go by."

But finally he started to get the message. "Are you sure that's how you feel?" he asked.

"I'm positive."

"Okay, but we've got to make a public statement. If we don't, it'll embarrass Jack."

"You could have done this two weeks ago so quickly and so quietly nobody ever would have known."

"We'll have to announce that Kramer's being up there will hurt your performance."

"Bullshit. No way he's gonna hurt my performance. I don't care if the Queen of England's up there. That's not the point."

So we went on about that for awhile. In the end we agreed that Larry would read a statement at the beginning of the program explaining why Gene Scott was doing the color instead of Jack Kramer. That wasn't a totally satisfactory solution, but at least the matter was settled. By now the match was less than a day and a half away.

I'd begun preparing for Riggs seriously the day after I lost that TV match to Evert. At Hilton Head I got into a routine I always try to use when I'm playing night tennis. I forced myself to stay up late and sleep in until ten or eleven in the morning so that when the match came around my body would really be used to that time schedule, to having its high point from seven to ten o'clock at night, when I really feel the best. It seems like a small thing, but when I want to get psyched up I spend a lot of time on the details, to make sure everything's perfect.

I did a lot of lifting weights for my legs and knees. I

217

did a lot of that and it really helped. My legs were so strong the night of the match I couldn't believe it. I took good care of myself and got a lot of rest. And I got my head together.

Pete Collins, the resident pro at Hilton Head, made himself available to me anytime I wanted to hit. He and I had two sessions a day of about an hour each. I didn't overdo it because I felt it was too late to start really training hard. Pete and I mainly just rallied a lot, and I tried to concentrate on each shot, each swing of the racket, to get a good rhythm going. Sometimes we hit just to see how long we could keep the ball in play, and I got very patient inside. When I get that way I can stay on the base line all day if I have to.

That was going to be my alternate strategy—the base-line game. I wanted to be able to mix it up—go in some, stay back a little—but what I wanted to do especially at the start was to go in and put away some volleys because I thought that would break Bobby down faster psychologically. I practiced a lot of volleying and a lot of lateral movement and up-and-back movement. I felt pretty sure he didn't realize how quick I was or how good a volley I had. He knew, of course, I had a good volley—for a girl. But I thought my volley was strong in anybody's department, men's or women's, and I was counting on him underestimating me in that respect.

I hit a lot of service returns and overheads, especially overheads because I knew he was going to throw up a lot of lobs and wait for me to miss a few. But I felt that if I could either run them down or put them away, he'd be done. Finished. Pete was fantastically patient. He must have hit two hundred lobs a day.

I didn't practice my service very much because I'd already decided I wouldn't serve very hard to him. He's at his best when he can counterpunch against his opponent's power, and so I'd decided not to give him any power at all. I did practice changing my service all the time, going from a hard, flat serve to a slice serve to a topspin to a twist. It's not easy to do with any consistency because it takes a real sense of touch and accuracy. So as far as my service went, I thought in these terms: keep changing it around and serve the ball into his body a lot. I felt that was going to be important: to serve into him, then go wide—make him go exceptionally wide—to always keep him off balance, because he's the type of player who relies on his own balance to keep the rally under control.

Finally, I worked on keeping my shots to his backhand side—his weak side—then hitting very sharply to his forehand. Again, the idea was to confuse him, run him around the court, keep him from getting control.

Marilyn Barnett, who'd come in from L.A. late in the week, Dick Butera, and I left Hilton Head for Houston on the Sunday night before the match—Larry was already there—and I swear, it was like we were all going off to war or something. It was very upbeat, but very eerie, too, like we were going someplace we might not return from. I really didn't know what to expect.

My parents arrived the next day and we all stayed together in a hotel about fifteen minutes from the Astrodome. I tried not to change my routine at all from what it had been in Hilton Head. The only real difference—except for a big press conference on Tuesday and that business with Roone Arledge on Wednesday—was that a practice court had been set up in the Astrodome parking lot under a plastic bubble and that's where we went to hit, for two hours a night, until the match.

The days went quickly, and then it was Thursday.

I got up around noon, had breakfast, and started eating candy. I ate candy all day. My parents stopped by, along with Larry, Dick, Marilyn Barnett, and Dennis Van der Meer, my coach from Berkeley, who was going to be my official "second" that night. Wednesday night Dennis, Pete Collins, and I had looked at the Court–Riggs tape again and had discussed my strategy —the kinds of things I've already mentioned—and we went over that some more. Then I got antsy. I left my room and went downstairs and around the corner to a supermarket, and shopped. Got some cheeses, apples, other snack stuff, and I'm sure it blew the minds of the other customers.

The rest of the day I just lay around the hotel room, mostly in my favorite position—on the floor with my feet up on the bed— talking to whoever happened to wander by. I listened to "Jesus Christ Superstar" on the radio, and read through some of the hundreds of telegrams that had been pouring in throughout the week.

About four in the afternoon, I went over to the Astrodome with Dick and Marilyn. It was only the second time I'd actually been on the field, and it's really important for me to get the feel of a place, the atmosphere—like I do at Wimbledon every year—by just walking around and absorbing the sense of where I am. I tried to let the Astrodome sink in really fast. Like, triple time. I went down to the court, which was laid out approximately where second base is, and looked up and thought, "This is it, man. You've got to get used to this place."

It was such a huge building that the feeling of space was weird, not like a tennis stadium at all. But the room around the court, between the court and the $100 ground-level seats, wasn't very much at all, especially behind the base lines. And straight up—there was this ring of lights hanging over the center of the court and I knew right away if a lob ever got up in there, forget it.

I had the Astrodome people take me into the locker

room and show me where my brother, Randy, dresses when the San Francisco Giants play in Houston. I had specifically asked for the visitors' dressing room for that reason. They showed me Randy's locker and it turned out the number, 22, was the same as my birth date. A good omen. It also turned out later it was the wrong locker.

I did an interview with Frank Gifford for ABC, and finally went out and hit two-on-one against Pete Collins and Dennis Van der Meer. Nothing fancy. I was just trying to get used to the court. This was the biggest problem both Bobby and I had. The court was the same one we'd played on in the bubble, but out there it was laid over asphalt and played very fast. Inside, it was stretched over a plywood basketball court and was really dead in spots, and slow all over. It took us both a while to adjust.

After I finished hitting, I had a shower and changed clothes, then had a real training-table pre-match meal of Gatorade and candy. By then the people were starting to come in, the band was playing, the lights were turned on bright for the television cameras—and the pressure of the whole thing finally got to me. It hit me in a very strange way. I had my usual pre-match tension, of course, but, beyond that, in the hour or so before the match I felt more utterly alone than I ever had in my life. I just got totally wrapped up in my own thoughts. I remembered all the hassles and the headaches of the early years of the Slims tour, and I thought about how far we'd come in such a short time. It really came home to me—hard—that if I lost to Riggs much of what we'd won for ourselves might go right out the window. I'd sensed it before, but now I knew this match was one of the big three in my life—the others were against Maria Bueno in the 1966 Wimbledon finals and against Chris Evert at Forest Hills in 1971—

221

in each case where a defeat would just about erase everything that I'd done before. Everybody else in Houston was having a ball, but that hour before Bobby and I actually stepped on the court was probably the most agonizing one of my life.

I finally had to get away. I knew Virginia Slims was having a party upstairs and I said to Dick Butera, "Let's go. I've got to get away from this." Well, it was jaw-drop time all the way—in the elevator, in the public restaurant we had to walk through to get to the Slims' suite, and then at the party. Nobody could believe I was there just an hour before the match—and I hate cocktail parties—but I needed something, anything, to get rid of the tension and that awful feeling of loneliness.

No luck. At the party, something I'd felt all week in Houston really hit home: a lot of the other women players didn't really think I could win. Some of them had even bet against me, and most of the rest felt I was about to go to the guillotine, or something. And that really hurt me, gave me a lot to think about.

I only stayed a few minutes.

Back downstairs, one of the last people I talked to before the match began was Bud Collins, the Boston tennis writer and good friend who had taken Karen Hantze and me out to dinner after our first Wimbledon doubles title twelve years before.

"Hi, Bud," I said. "How'd you bet?"

"I went with Bobby."

Terrific.

Then the extravaganza began. Bobby was wheeled out in that ridiculous rickshaw, and I was carried onto the court in one of those throne-like litters, a little item I'd checked out carefully beforehand. I'm terrified of heights, and wobbling around four feet off the ground is just about my limit. Then Bobby presented me with a gigantic Sugar Daddy—about the size of a tennis racket—and I reciprocated by giving him Larimore Hustle, a little Male Chauvinist Piglet brought in for the occasion. (Bobby's middle name is Larimore. In answer to many queries, Larimore Hustle got lost in the excitement after the match, was found late that night huddled in a corner of the Astrodome, and now lives on a farm in Oklahoma—assuming the price of pork hasn't dictated another fate.)

When we walked on the court to warm up, I couldn't believe the crowd. The Astrodome wasn't sold out, but I'll guarantee you nobody else could have gotten in and had a good seat for a tennis match. Now it really was like a circus, or a baseball game, or maybe even a heavyweight title fight. Balloons, bands, noise, the works. People were shouting, "Right on, Billie Jean," or, "Go, Bobby," from the moment we entered and even well into the match. I loved it. Just the way a tennis crowd ought to be, everywhere. No indifference. I doubt if there was a neutral person in the whole Astrodome.

But once the match started, everything was straight. No gamesmanship, no hustle, no nothing except tennis. At the rules meeting the day before, when we'd decided on things like the special ten-minute injury time out, I'd been emphatic about that. I told Bobby, "I don't care what you do before we walk on the court, but once that match starts you don't walk over to my table, you don't talk to me, you don't touch me . . ."

"Aaaw, Billie Jean, you don't care if I . . ."

". . . Nothing. We're gonna play a match, straight tennis."

I didn't want there to be any doubts at all about the match. It had to be on the level, and it was. When we were warming up, he called me over for a chat and I waved him away. I knew that if the match started turn-

223

ing in my favor he'd try anything, and I wanted to shut him off before he could begin.

Just before the match began I told myself, "Okay, this is it. Take each point by itself and don't rush things." Geez, just thinking of that moment months later I still get nervous and start to sweat.

I served first and won the first game of the match, and I knew right away this wasn't going to be a repeat of the Margaret Court thing. I also couldn't believe how slow he was. I thought he was faking it. He had to be. At the change after the first game I asked Dennis, "He's putting me on, right?"

Dennis assured me I was seeing the real thing, but I think Riggs did coast the first three or four games, though, trying to figure me out and at the same time not give away all of his wonderful secrets.

He broke my service in the fifth game when I missed a backhand volley by two inches, and took a 3–2 lead. I thought the next game was the most crucial of the match. If he held he'd be up 4–2 and I'd have to win three of the next four games to get back even and deuce the set at 5–all. If I broke back right away it would help my confidence and also let him know he was in for a real fight. Up to that point I'd been trying to make my shots too good, but I realized I just didn't have to go for the lines every time. He was slow, he couldn't hit with a lot of pace, and I could take the net any time I wanted. I just didn't need to make that good a shot. And so I calmed down, broke his service immediately to even the first set at 3–3—and then really got into it.

I was kind of shocked because I thought he would be a lot better than he was. He didn't have a big service, and his spins—"The ones that always get the girls"—weren't that great either. And I was absolutely right about him not realizing how quick I was at the net or how well I could volley. Five of the first six times he tried to pass me off his backhand side I just ran the ball down and—bam—volleyed away a winner. Near the end of the first set there was a great point where he hit wide and deep to my forehand, then wide and deep to my backhand. I ran 'em both down, and on the second shot I flopped up a base-line lob and got right back into the point. He didn't believe I could run down those kinds of shots.

I concentrated hard on winning that first set and when I did—on a double fault by Bobby—I knew he was in big trouble. That meant he'd have to play at least four tough sets to win the match, probably more hard competitive tennis than he'd played in years. I felt I was in pretty good shape, and that things were going my way.

Larry wasn't quite sure, however, and he cost Dick Butera $5,000.

There was a lot of gambling on the match, of course, official and unofficial, and Bobby was covering a lot of the unofficial money himself. The Las Vegas odds, courtesy of Nick the Greek, were 5 to 2, Riggs. Bobby was offering 8 to 5, a little bit shorter. Butera wanted to bet $5,000 on me at 2 to 1 and Bobby agreed, in a deal they made with a nod of their heads after the first game of the match.

At the end of the first set, Bobby offered Dick another $5,000—this time even money. But Larry was wary. Against anybody else he would have been confident I had things under control, but something didn't feel right to him. He knew Bobby wasn't hustling any more, but he also knew Bobby maybe could play better tennis if he had a little more incentive—like another $5,000 on the line—and he told Butera not to put any more money down. And he didn't. I don't know how much money changed hands that night, but it was a bundle.

About midway through the second set, I knew that the match was mine if I could just keep up the pace. But I didn't let up because I'd gotten into trouble too many times before thinking I had a match won before it was over.

Everything that I thought would work before the match did work. I played conservatively those last two sets and always waited for the right shot before I came in. I thought he'd be running everything down and keep throwing up lobs the whole time, but he just didn't do it. His backhand never got any better, I missed just one overhead the entire three sets, and at the end I was playing with complete confidence.

On match point I threw my racket in the air and just when I looked down I saw him finish his jump over the net. He came over to congratulate me, and then he was really nice. He said, "You're too good," and that was it.

Up to that point I'd really had mixed feelings about Riggs. I always liked him personally but I had also resented a lot of the statements he had made, if only in jest, before the match. When it was over, though, I kind of felt sorry for him, and I put my arm around him. Then all hell broke loose.

I don't know what the Astrodome people thought. I guess they figured that because it was a tennis match the people would be dignified when it was over. They weren't. They were great. George Foreman, the world heavyweight champion, was supposed to make the presentations, but fat chance. I got bombed from all sides. Larry was trying to protect me. Marilyn was trying to protect me. Marilyn! She must weigh 100 pounds. She had bruises all over her body from the crush. So did Larry. So did I. Larry finally lifted me on a little table so I could show off the trophy. Then a security guard arrived and Foreman was able to give me the check. I remember looking down at the "$100,000" written on it and thinking that looked pretty funny. I'd never seen a check that big before—made out to me.

I got to the press conference first—I guess Bobby went to comb his hair forward in that funny way he does. I had a beer. I couldn't wait to have a beer. Then I sat there with my shoes off with all those microphones around and looking at all those faces and thinking about all the past things that had happened to get me to where I was that night. I was so relieved. I was just happy it was over.

That night Jerry Perenchio held a party at the Astroworld Hotel but I was whacked out. I did a five-minute walk-through, then got out of there and went back to my hotel and ate ice cream with Larry and my parents, read some more telegrams, and went to bed. Ten weeks of getting psyched up for one night of tennis and then, boom, it was all over.

The match was tough, mentally and physically. I've played better matches, but under the circumstances I played as well as I possibly could, and so, I think, did Bobby. I'm sure a lot of players who watched the match are convinced they can beat Riggs too, so what's the big deal? Well, sure they can beat him—on Court 50 at their home club with three people watching. But let 'em try it before 40 million people and I think things would be different.

As far as the importance of the match, it proved just two things: First, that a woman *can* beat a man. Second, that tennis can be a big-time sport, and will, once it gets into the hands of the people who know how to promote it.

My personal opinion of Riggs? Well—now, after the match, I feel he's a very nice guy, actually a kind person who loves the spotlight and loves to hustle. And I wish him well. There was some talk of a rematch, but I can say without any hesitation that I'll never play him again. It was a one-shot deal and I think I proved my point.

6–4, 6–3, 6–3.

10

The Last Word—
But Not Really

IT's pretty ironic, I think, that the one thing that motivates champion athletes more than anything else is the fear of failing. On the way up, there's always that insidious nagging feeling that you're not going to quite make it, that in the crunch you're going to come up just a little bit short; and once you reach the top there's the absolute dread of the day when it's all going to end. You can never win enough titles, or money, or awards, because people always expect you to do it just one more time, and, of course, you come to expect it of yourself. Tennis may be pretty insignificant in the overall picture, but for those few hours during a match it really is life or death. Each victory is like a new breath of air and each defeat takes something away from you that can never be replaced.

Maybe that's why I've never been able to enjoy a particular victory for very long, or any other single accomplishment. I've been asked many times what my feelings were when I had those two $100,000 prize-money years, or when I was named Sportswoman of the Year, or when I beat Bobby Riggs. My answer is always the same—relief. Nothing else. That indicates a

It would be nice if every loss and every victory were equal, but unfortunately they're not. Victory is fleeting, but losing is forever, and that makes all the difference. Defeat is something I just can't seem to get rid of. It never leaves my insides.

----

pretty restless mentality, I guess, but my happiness comes from trying to reach a goal much more than from actually attaining it. Because once I've done something it's over—finished—and there is always something else to get on with. People assume that my first big win, over Margaret Smith at Wimbledon in 1962, must certainly have been a thrill. But it wasn't, not really. It was important to my career, but it just wasn't a thrill. When the match was over I must have tossed my racket in the air—I usually do—but the enjoyment of even that win was almost literally over by the time the racket landed. I enjoyed that victory for maybe ten seconds, and that's the truth. I mean, I'd won. Fine, yay, but then it was behind me forever.

A couple of years ago on New Year's Eve I wrote down for myself something about winning and losing. It was awful and I'd never want to see it in print, but the essence of it was that all the hassling I'd gone through, all the defeats, all that agonizing fighting to my last breath were, in the end, made worthwhile by those moments of triumph, even if they didn't last very long. I felt that I was never free from the demands that were imposed on me and, more important, really didn't want to be, because I could always think about and look forward to those few seconds when the racket would be sailing triumphantly in the air again.

There's something else to say, though. It would be nice if every loss and every victory were equal, but unfortunately they're not. It is true that victory is fleeting, but losing is forever, and that makes all the difference. I've said that I carried around the memory of that loss to Margaret Smith in the 1963 Wimbledon finals for years, and I really did. Defeat is something I just can't seem to get rid of. It never leaves my insides.

The best players, I think, are always the ones who remember their losses because they remember the pain and they hate it. Rod Laver is a lot like that, although he rarely shows it outwardly. I remember in 1970 when he was at the absolute peak of his game—he'd won the Grand Slam the year before—and then he was upset at Wimbledon in the fourth round by Roger Taylor. The next day I saw him at Queen's Club where we all practice during the Wimbledon Fortnight and I'll never forget the look on his face. It was as though someone had ripped the guts from his belly. And, of course, in a sense that had happened. I tried to talk to him, but he didn't want to say very much. He didn't have to tell me anything. I knew he'd remember that match for a long, long time.

I think the hardest thing in the world to accept, for a player who really wants to be Number One, is the fact that he or she doesn't have what it takes. It must be absolutely crushing. But no one should ever accept that fact too easily. It's important, I think, really important, to push yourself to the edge of your own limit just to find out where that limit is. Arthur Ashe, for example, is afraid of failure like we all are, but he won't try to be Number One because I believe in all kindness that deep down he feels he can't be the best.

Even after he won the first-ever U.S. Open in 1968 I think he knew—after you've played enough years and enough tournaments you're your own best judge. And so Arthur won't really try to find out. It's better, I think, to push yourself and fail because at least you'll have tried. When Arthur's sixty-five and says to himself, "I gave it all I had," he'll be fooling himself, because I don't think Arthur has done that. And he'll never know whether he could have reached the very top.

I expect to win every time I step on the tennis court and I'm truly surprised when I don't. That attitude, I'm pretty sure, goes all the way back. It was already there the day I made that (I suspect) less than marvelous catch as the hotshot ten-year-old shortstop on the Houghton Park girls' softball team. When the other kids congratulated me and patted me on the back, I just couldn't handle it. I turned red, I hung my head—the whole bit. I didn't think about it at all because I'd expected to make that kind of catch and double up that runner at third. Big deal.

I've been successful in tennis basically because of something I had nothing to do with—my talent. I was born with the physical and—to some degree—the mental ability to hit a tennis ball with accuracy and power, and that's all there is to it. Maybe I can be praised a little for using that talent, I believe, to its fullest, but not at all for having it in the first place. When everything is right on and I know I'm playing my absolute best tennis, I really don't believe there are very many players who can come close to me. Not Evert, Goolagong, Court, or anybody else. I'm sure they all feel the same way about themselves, too, and I'm sure that Laver and Gonzalez felt like that when they were at the absolute peak of their games. On my very best days I have this fantastic, utterly unself-conscious feeling of invincibility.

I still get that charge out of winning, and even from just hitting one great shot. If I didn't get that charge and suddenly found myself asking, "Is this really worth it?" that would probably be a good reason to stop playing. But that hasn't happened, not yet. Something inside keeps pushing me to go on. That restlessness, drive, motivation, or whatever you want to call it hasn't gone away yet. I'm not sure how to explain it; except I have a funny feeling it's probably the same thing that makes people go crazy too.

The more I play the more I'm amazed by this desire, that I and other top players apparently have, to succeed and accomplish something. Ken Rosewall has been around now for over twenty years. Laver's been a world-class player for fifteen, Court for thirteen. I've been playing internationally since 1961, and I don't know why I still want to be Number One. Maybe there's some basic insecurity beyond the simple fear of losing. All I know is that it's a part of me and I can't repress it. I can't say, "Okay, I'm not gonna go to work today." No way. I still love to play; every time I walk on the court I feel the need to prove myself all over again. Being Number One isn't everything to me, but for those few hours on the court it's way ahead of whatever's in second place.

Sometimes I find it hard to motivate myself. I've got to have a goal. If I start to play and find myself asking, "What does this match really mean?" I know I'm in trouble. Long-range goals are the best. In those years when Wimbledon was the most important thing in the world to me, just thinking about the place was enough to get me on the practice court months and months before the tournament.

Short-range goals are a little tougher to figure. I get psyched up pretty automatically before key matches in major championships—like I did before I played Evert at Forest Hills in 1971—but doing it week in and week out on the circuit is a little trickier. Sometimes I need some outside help.

In 1972, for example, Larry helped put together a tournament in Albany, California, near the end of the year. It was a last-minute deal and a lot of things went wrong, but overall I thought it was worthwhile because it was an extra tournament and gave us another $20,000 to play for. Well, I don't understand it, but Frankie Durr ran down the thing in the papers, which I didn't appreciate, and so did my old friend Julie Heldman, whom I happened to play in the quarter finals.

As we walked on the court, Julie said, "This has just got to be the worst-run tournament of the year. Larry really messed up."

"What did you say?"

"Do you think it's been a great tournament?"

"Julie," I said, "there've been worse and there've been better, but this deal's sure better than not playing."

I was furious at her for running down the tournament but even more pissed because she'd jumped on Larry. He was cool, as usual. He just sat there calm and collected and kept telling me not to get steamed up but I couldn't help it. Julie and I spun the racket for service, and I mustered up just about the dirtiest look I could—and she wilted. I worked my buns off that match. Just played great. Julie tried everything in the book and I had an answer for it all. She won exactly two games.

That's a real short-term goal.

(It was also a perfect example of the kind of rage Pancho Gonzalez mastered a long time ago. He can explode and humiliate everyone in sight—the linesman, the umpire, the crowds—but five minutes later he's concentrating as though nothing happened. I'm often not quite that good at it because I sometimes tend to carry my anger longer and if I'm not careful it can affect my game. Against Julie that night, though, I found the perfect combination.)

I like to play on emotion, any emotion at all. The best days are those when I can feel the excitement of the crowd—it doesn't have to be a big crowd, either, although they're the best—and get a sense of the drama. There are times, however, when everything comes up just flat no matter how much I goad myself, and when that happens I have to force myself to just hang in the match until something—anything—happens to set off a spark and get me on the track.

But good tennis also requires a lot of self-discipline and sometimes the two things—emotion and discipline —get in the way of each other.

It's been said many times before that one of the real marks of a champion is not the ability to win when you're playing well, but the ability to pull out matches when you're playing badly. And raising your game that essential notch or two when your emotions are asking you "Why bother with all this nonsense?" is a pretty difficult trick. Sometimes I'm successful at that, sometimes I'm not.

I guess I'm pretty disciplined, but it's not really my bag. I hate regimentation, and training has always been difficult for me. I hate to lift weights even though I know it helps my legs. Jogging for the sake of jogging bores me to tears. I love to stay up late although I know I need my sleep. I go crazy around candy bars and ice cream even though my weight has always been borderline. I love to read and go to the movies, but I know that's bad for my eyes. I'd like to be able to just play competition tennis and not have to worry about any of the other stuff at all. If I hadn't been raised by parents with a pretty strong sense of discipline themselves, I would have been hopeless, absolutely hopeless.

Because I'm emotional, I'm not really consistent when compared with players like Margaret Court and Nancy Gunter, whose games don't seem to vary a beat day in and day out. I try, God knows, but consistency is just not a part of my makeup either. For example, I have a lot of oh-how-insignificant-tennis-is-when-people-are-starving periods. I'm not sorry I think about things like that, but if I start doing it in the middle of a tennis tournament, it can be pretty bad news. I think maybe the worst experience was at Forest Hills in 1972 the day of my quarter-final match with Virginia Wade. I'd played okay the first week, but nothing sensational, and I was a little bit worried. Then, the night before the quarters I told Larry—announced to him—"Everything's fine. Whatever was missing is back again. No problems."

Just before Virginia and I walked on the court, however, they had this tribute to the murdered Israeli Olympians and I was shattered. Hit bottom. I started thinking about what human beings do to each other and I began questioning why I was about to play a game in the middle of it all. I had to work hard to stay in the match that day, and I really wasn't with it very much at all.

Being emotional also works against concentration, sometimes. I like the feeling of playing every point like it's forever, but occasionally I get so carried away with the idea that I'm just in another world. Sometimes I won't even keep track of the score—which drives my doubles partners crazy—and at other times my mind wanders so far that I'm in a hole before I'm really aware of what's happening. I'm sometimes almost envious of a player like Chris Evert who has the ability to concentrate on tennis one hundred percent almost all the time and because of that she never plays below a certain level. Never.

After Chrissie's first Wimbledon in 1972 she talked

about how strange it felt to travel all over the world and not really see any of it—except for tennis courts and hotels. It just never occurred to her there was anything else to do in London except play tennis. She didn't care whether she shopped three days of the Fortnight or that she didn't see Buckingham Palace or pick up a pair of Gucci shoes. She was right on, and that's why I think she might be a great player some day. Buckingham Palace will always be there and you can pick up Guccis anywhere, but you only get a few chances to win at Wimbledon.

When I walk out on the court for any match, the first thing I do is try to get a sense of the atmosphere —the vibes. Next, as I did in Houston, I size up the arena and try to get comfortable in it, try to get a proper perspective. This isn't as routine as it sounds, even in a reasonably familiar place. People sitting off the ends of the court in white shirts, for example, are often a problem because the ball gets lost in that kind of background. Indoors, where more and more of our tournaments are being played, I know that something like the height of the ceiling will affect my perspective on lobs. The lighting might be erratic and so I check for dark spots. If the artificial court is laid over a plywood base, I'll look for dead spots and check its general resiliency. Just getting the feel of a court is very important. At Wimbledon, the lush greenery everywhere makes it a very cozy place to play, and the geometry of everything from Centre Court to the last field court is so perfect that I always can get a nice, squared-off sense of where I am. At Forest Hills, though, the fences behind the field courts are at an angle to the base line so that there may be twenty feet behind the court at one side line and twenty-five feet behind the court at the other. That's enough to throw off anybody's game.

When I've finished with that kind of thing, I review

in my mind the basic strategy I want to use that day. My best style of play is the serve-and-volley game, of course, but sometimes I might decide to stay on the base line, just to show my opponent—or, more important, myself—I can hit ground strokes too. If I need the work, I might decide to concentrate only on putting topspin on my shots and hitting with depth. The possibilities are limitless.

Sometimes I get thinking about too many things before a match, or even—really bad—during it. I always like to be able to sense the crowd, and that's important, but sometimes I get hung up on what's running through the umpire's mind, or what the linesmen and lineswomen are thinking, or even what the ball boys and ball girls are thinking. God, sometimes the kids look so scared and nervous that I feel like saying, "It's all right. Don't be nervous. You're doing fine." And for a player to get preoccupied with things like that in the middle of a match, she's got to be out of her mind.

I'm a music nut, and I sing to myself all the time on the court, especially if there's a song that relates to my immediate situation—whether I'm happy or sad, or winning or losing, or feeling good or feeling lousy. I'll go over the lyrics, or at least some fragments, or just let the tunes drift through my mind. I like soul the best. And I love Simon and Garfunkel's old stuff like "Sounds of Silence." Both the music and lyrics, the whole thing. When I first heard Janis Joplin sing "Freedom's just another word for nothin' left to lose," it just really gassed me out. It became a Centre Court standard. I can't stand Sinatra, but I like the lyrics of "My Way." And some of Carole King's stuff—"So Far Away" and "You've Got a Friend" especially—is just perfect, right on the mark. And "Mother Freedom," by Bread. Fantastic. ". . . Freedom get movin', never gonna stop till everybody's groovin' on love for one another." It blows my mind!

When I'm doing that—singing on the court—I know I'm playing good tennis. This isn't as crazy as it sounds. It means that I'm not thinking consciously about tennis and that as far as the plain mechanics of hitting the ball go, my mind is at a sort of zero point. Neutral. Because instinct is everything, and that's exactly how I want it to be. If I'm thinking too much during a match, it's a dead giveaway that something isn't quite right with my game.

Instinct is what allows me to make the instantaneous connection between knowing what I ought to do on a certain shot and actually doing it. It's sort of a short-hand connection between the brain—the unconscious brain—and the body, because when I'm playing on instinct alone I have no idea what I'm doing physically on any of my shots. I really don't. I've been told, for example, that I hit my backhand, which I feel is one of my best shots, in a very strange way. I agree, but only because I've seen films of myself. At the time I'm actually hitting one, I have no idea what my body's doing. I know my backswing is normal and that my follow-through isn't too unusual, but somewhere in between I do this sort of odd thing with my wrist that allows me both to disguise the direction of the shot very nicely, and to be able to come over the ball or to slice it, or to hit it flat, whichever's right.

It's really amazing. I've asked a lot of the other players to analyze what exactly it is they do during a shot: "How do you hit your forehand?" And the better they are, the more likely they are to not know the answer.

Knowing that I'm playing totally by instinct gives me tremendous self-confidence. I'm sure, just positive, that since my instincts are basically good, nothing can go wrong. What I do think about on those super days are things like my patterns—what shots I'm going to hit in a certain situation—my own movements, and how I'm playing generally. I don't worry about how I'm hitting the ball, and I hardly notice my opponent at all. It's like I'm out there by myself. I've talked with Laver and Rosewall about this, and even Court a little, and on their great days their attitude is exactly the same. I concentrate only on the ball in relationship to the face of my racket, which is a full-time job anyway, since no two balls ever come over the net the same way. I appreciate what my opponent is doing, but in a very detached, abstract way, like an observer in the next room. I see her moving to her left or right, but it's almost as though there weren't any real opponent, as though I didn't know—and certainly didn't care—whom I was playing against.

When I'm in that kind of state (and sometimes even when I'm not), I feel that tennis is an art form that's capable of moving both the players and the audience —at least a knowledgeable audience—in emotional, almost sensual ways. Tennis is a personal expression on my part, certainly the most complete and maybe the only way I can express myself. When I'm performing at my absolute best, I think that some of the euphoria that I feel must be transmitted to the audience. That may be a pretty feeble definition of art, but for me, the rhythms of tennis are very similar to the movements of a ballet, and the emotion that comes from a great match or even a single great shot is like the emotion you feel when you hear a moving piece of music.

There's a real conflict within me sometimes between what might be called the aesthetics of tennis and the need to win. In certain situations I'm really tempted to try and hit a flashier, more fun shot than is smart. But I hate to lose so much that I involuntarily revert to the percentage shots and patterns that I know will work best. It kills me to admit it, but I'm a duller player because of my need to win.

I think Torben Ulrich of Denmark must be the only world-class player who truly and honestly doesn't care if he wins or loses. He's into aesthetics one hundred percent and I suspect he'd be quite happy playing without a marked-off court or even a net. Along the same line, sort of, I once heard of another pretty good player who was so into the mental side of tennis—he was a coach too, and that was really his first love—that if he was playing against somebody with a weak backhand, for example, he'd practically stop the match in order to show his opponent what he was doing wrong. Then he'd give him all backhands—setups—and be absolutely delighted when the guy started teeing off on them and eventually won the match.

I think I'll concentrate on winning, for a few more years, at least, but there is something to be said for the aesthetic approach to the game. If I didn't get a pure, abstract pleasure from just hitting that ball solidly, time after time, there's no way I'd continue playing. Who in her right mind would live out of a suitcase for thirteen years or more, check in and out of hotels and motels constantly, and go through all the other daily hassles, if in the very end, she just didn't like to play and to constantly test herself against the best players in the world? In this respect, it's impossible to satisfy me totally. I know I'm a perfectionist, that no matter how well I play I'll always feel I could have played a lot better. Other players have asked me whether I was ever satisfied, whether I had just once walked off the court and been able to say that was the absolute best I could do.

And the answer has honestly been "No."

The perfect match would be one in which I won every point and did that by hitting every shot exactly how and where I wanted. The real challenge, the real fun, is to see how close I can come to that.

A couple of years ago Stan Smith beat Jan Kodes, 6–0, 6–1, in a tournament in Barcelona. Did he feel he could ever play a better match? In his life?

Stan said he hadn't really thought about it. Then he

thought about it. "Y'know," he said, "there were some upsetting things about the match. I missed a couple of backhand returns, and Jan passed me a couple of times."

That's what I'm talking about. Stan had come so close to perfection that day that the frustration of knowing that it really was impossible was more real than maybe if he'd played the worst match of his life. He knew there would always be a few shots—a mis-hit volley, a forehand without quite enough topspin—to keep the perfect match out of reach forever. I sometimes think that the creativity needed for great tennis comes directly from this kind of frustration.

The perfect *shot* is another matter. They don't come along very often, but when they do, they're great. It gives me a marvelous feeling of almost perfect joy—especially if I can pull one off on the last shot of the match.

I can almost feel it coming. It usually happens on one of those days when everything is just right, when the crowd is large and enthusiastic and my concentration is so perfect it almost seems as though I'm able to transport myself beyond the turmoil on the court to some place of total peace and calm. I know where the ball is on every shot, and it always looks as big and as well-defined as a basketball. Just a huge thing that I couldn't miss if I wanted to. I've got perfect control of the match, my rhythm and movements are excellent, and everything's just in total balance. That's the setup.

Usually, that is, because the most satisfying shot I've ever hit, strangely enough, came on a day when I had to really scramble the whole afternoon. But it was an important match—the 1972 Wimbledon final against Evonne Goolagong. Neither one of us was very sharp that day, and I was really playing just to win the match as best I could and get off the court. Then, on match point, it happened. I'd been going down the line on my

backhand all afternoon—that's the percentage shot—
but there was always just enough of a crosswind to hold
up the ball long enough for Evonne to run them down.
So I waited, and I told myself that on match point I'd
do just the opposite and bomb the thing crosscourt. I
served. She returned down the line to my backhand,
and I just snapped a short, topspin shot that I knew immediately was a winner. Then I threw my racket up in
the air—I'd planned to be demure and take it all in
stride—and I thought, "Thank God that out of the
whole bloody match I hit one shot that was just absolutely right."

The perfect shot. It's just an, "Aaaahhh"—all those
years of preparation, the moments of losing and of mis-
hitting the ball, all those nights as a kid when I stayed
out when the sun was going down until I couldn't see
the ball anymore—that indescribable feeling of meeting
the ball right in the old pocket just the way you planned
it. . . . No, you didn't plan anything, not really. It just
happened.

It can happen anytime, and like the shot against
Goolagong, it can really catch you by surprise. But
most players have a favorite shot or two that gives them
a bigger kick than the others. The one shot I love to
make is when my opponent lobs over me and I run
back and pass her with a backhand. I love it, especially
when I get her wrong-footed. I can always see my opponent on that shot—not really see her but sense where
she is, and I really hide my backhand well. Like, I'll
fake it down the line and snap it crosscourt, or I'll wait
just long enough for her to think I've got to go crosscourt and then I'll go *boom* with it down the line. I love
to cut loose on that. It's such a free feeling, like that
film thing they always do in slow motion, where the two
young people are running toward each other, that feeling of putting everything together and of being in perfect harmony.

But it doesn't have to be that one favorite shot, or even a shot on a crucial point. I remember a drop shot I hit against Nancy Gunter in Indianapolis one year that really didn't mean a thing as far as our match was concerned, but it was one of *those* shots and I turned absolutely cold inside. I got chills and goose pimples and my heart was pounding—over one single drop shot.

That perfect moment happens in all sports. In basketball, it might be that split-second hesitation just before a player gets off a jump shot that you know is gonna go swish. In baseball, players say they can't feel the ball on the bat at all when they've hit a home run, but they know, they just know.

Whenever I get to talking about drugs, I always say, "I get high just by hitting a backhand," and it's always worth a laugh. But it's true, absolutely true. And more and more club players, even, are telling me, "I know what you mean. I hit *one* shot out of a whole doubles match the other day, and it was the greatest feeling."

It is, it is. It's a perfect combination of a violent action taking place in an atmosphere of total tranquility. My heart pounds, my eyes get damp, and my ears feel like they're wiggling, but it's also just totally peaceful. It's almost like having an orgasm—it's exactly like that. And when it happens I want to stop the match and grab the microphone and shout, *"That's* what it's all about." Because it is. It's not the big prize I'm going to win at the end of the match or anything else. It's just having done something that's totally pure and having experienced the perfect emotion, and I'm always a little sad that I can't communicate that feeling right at the moment it's happening. I can only hope the people realize what's going on.

So, after all the problems, the confrontations, the brief moments of victory and the lasting memories of defeats, has it all been worthwhile? Just no question.

I've made my mark and I know what it feels like to be the best in something. I think I've gotten a pretty fair deal.

But in the last few years, it's been harder and harder for me to limit my thinking to tennis. I honestly believe I could give up the competitive game in a minute and be happy just hitting around on a public parks court two or three times a week. I don't know. Maybe I'm kidding myself. Maybe when the time comes for me to retire I'll find out that I won't be happy as a weekend player after all, that what's turned me on all these years has really been the excitement and the constant challenge of big-time tennis.

I don't think that will happen, though. I really don't. I've already gotten a lot of satisfaction out of the other things I'm involved in—my magazine, my tennis camps, and the WTA, to name only a few. In a lot of ways I feel like I'm about to start out all over again, fresh, from scratch, and that the biggest part of my life is still in front of me. But I have no idea what the future will bring. None at all. Family life? Business? Publishing? Politics? Television? There are so many options it's almost frightening. But it's exciting to me, beyond words, that the options are there. Isn't that what the struggle has all been about?

So what does come next? Check back with me in about ten years.

Index

INDEX

251

INDEX

INDEX

Your Inner Child of the Past

🏵 **Once you were a child.**

🏵 **That child still lives within you—influencing and interfering in your adult life.**

🏵 **This book tells you HOW TO SOLVE YOUR ADULT EMOTIONAL PROBLEMS by recognizing, accepting and managing the feelings of YOUR INNER CHILD OF THE PAST.**

BY W. HUGH MISSILDINE, M.D.

AMONG THE NEW IDEAS AND FRESH APPROACHES IN THIS BOOK ARE:

- There are four people in every marriage bed
- Every "lone wolf" has an unwelcome companion
- There are times when it's all wrong to try to "do better"
- How the "command-resistance" cycle of childhood leads to adult sexual frustration
- How to be the right kind of parent to your "inner child of the past"
- Six rules for happy family life